AHEAD · OF · THE · GAME

GOLF

WARD LOCK

RICHARD BRADBEER ·

Series Editor Ian Morrison
Designed by Anita Ruddell
Illustrations by Bob Williams

Text set in 10/11pt Compugraphic Triumvirate by BP Integraphics, Bath, Avon
Printed and bound in Great Britain
at The Bath Press, Avon

British Library Cataloguing in Publication Data

Bradbeer, Richard
  Golf – (Ahead of the game)
  1. Golf
  I. Title II. Series
  796.352

  ISBN 0–7063–6884–3

Acknowledgements

The author and publishers would like to thank Colorsport for providing all photographs.

RICHARD BRADBEER

A senior staff instructor of the British PGA and North West coach to the English Golf Union, Richard Bradbeer is the senior professional at Royal Birkdale Golf Club. The Bradbeer family has been connected with golf for many years and Richard followed his father and uncle as the professional at Burnham, Somerset, before moving to Birkdale. In 1990 he became Captain of the PGA and thus followed his uncle Ernest who held the post some years earlier.

Frontispiece:
One of the 'golden boys' of British golf in the 1980s: Nick Faldo.

CONTENTS

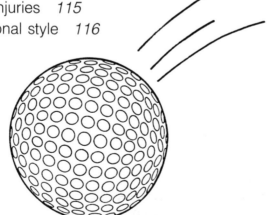

INTRODUCTION

Welcome to *Ahead of the Game*. If you read the first book in the series, *Play the Game*, you have no doubt familiarized yourself with the basic skills of this great game and are now ready to develop your game further. *Ahead of the Game* is designed to do just that.

We will help you understand the basics of a good hold, good stance and posture, and of course, a good golf swing. All very basic, you might think, but it is a crucial aspect of the game, and if you don't get it right at the outset then you will have all sorts of problems.

Once you have learned the basics of the golf swing and understand its movements, we will take you into various match situations that you will regularly come across. You will be guided through problems that crop up, such as 'Why have I started slicing?', or 'Suddenly I find I can't use a driver off the tee', and many more.

But don't think that you are going to be limited to the playing aspect of golf. There is more to this game than going on to the first tee and hitting a ball around for three or four hours. You have to be fit to do that regularly. So we will show you how to get, and keep, fit for golf. And for those of you who are injury prone, there is a useful guide on the prevention and/or cure of golfing injuries.

Finally, after you have been given a thorough training in the skills of golf, there is a chapter devoted to the different styles of the leading professionals.

You may find areas in the book where we have repeated key points. These are ones that must be hammered home to every golfer and that is the purpose of their repetition. By the time you get to the end of the book they will have become second nature to you.

o

The finest golfer of our life-time, and probably of all time, Jack Nicklaus.

GOLF

Whenever we teach you through *Ahead of the Game* you **must** practice regularly, and regular visits to your local professional are recommended. Refresher courses are never a bad thing in any walk of life. Golf is no different. If you have developed flaws in your game, your local pro will be able to identify them straight away. Let's be honest, finding flaws with yourself, whether it be on the golf course or in life in general, is never easy. Your golf professional will spot faults in your game instantly. If you want to become a better player then you must seek and take such advice.

Like most newcomers to golf you probably started on one of the many excellent municipal golf courses that can be found in most areas. Now that you are improving your standard of play, you may be considering joining a golf club. But please remember it often takes time and you are well advised to approach your local club now and complete an application form. After that, be patient.

However, you do not have to be a member of a golf club to approach its professional for lessons and advice. PGA professionals are available to everyone, not just club members. He is the man who can help you improve your game more than anybody. So seek his advice, and more importantly, listen to what he has to tell you. A combination of that and hard work and dedication will do nothing but turn you into a better golfer. We hope *Ahead of the Game* will play its part in helping your development.

Richard Bradbeer

ONE

THE BASICS
REVISED

All references assume you are right-handed.

Before we take you to the next stage in your advancement, it is best to go back to basics to reiterate the importance of the hold, stance, and swing.

Please don't think that because you have been playing golf for a while you can skip this section. This opening chapter is the most important one of the entire book. If you don't understand your clubs, how to hold the clubs, how to stand, or how to swing, then the rest of the book is redundant.

So, let's start with the golf club. You have up to 14 in your bag, but do you really understand them? You will know the difference between a wood and an iron, and that each has a head and a handle. But do you understand the club?

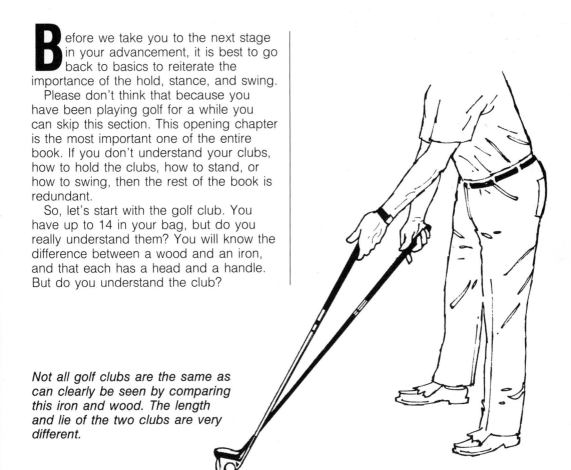

Not all golf clubs are the same as can clearly be seen by comparing this iron and wood. The length and lie of the two clubs are very different.

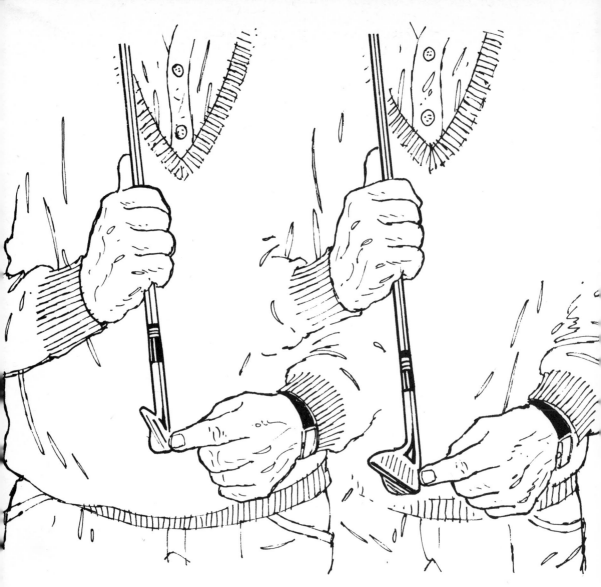

UNDERSTANDING · THE · CLUB

You are familiar with the *different* parts of the club; the handle, shaft, toe, face etc. But the important area is the leading edge, the bottom of the face which should be at right angles from the player to the ball-to-target area. This determines the loft on each club. You must develop a 'feel' for the leading edge of each club.

To appreciate the leading edge, stand opposite a player who has adopted a normal stance. Look at the club-head. As the club is taken back into the backswing, the face of the club gradually becomes visible to the onlooker. As it returns to the ball, you can clearly see how the leading edge is at a right angle to the ball-to-target line, and as the club-head follows through, all of the back of the club-head gradually becomes visible.

Right, so you now understand your club. Let's now look at the way you hold it.

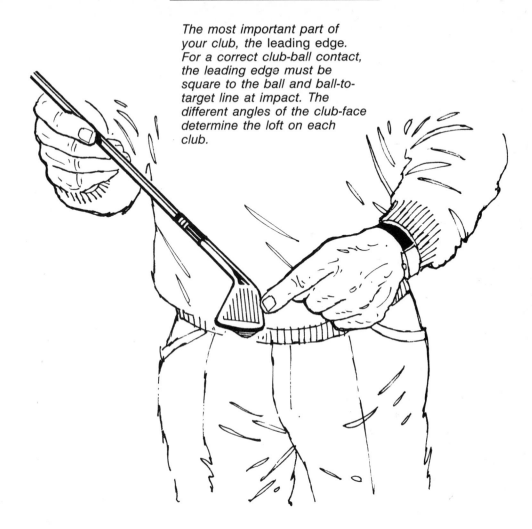

The most important part of your club, the leading edge. *For a correct club-ball contact, the leading edge must be square to the ball and ball-to-target line at impact. The different angles of the club-face determine the loft on each club.*

THE · HOLD

The hold, often referred to as the 'grip', is crucial. If you don't have a good hold, you can expect to encounter all sorts of problems.

To take a good hold put your left hand out as if you are about to shake hands. Place the club diagonally across the palm of the hands and apply pressure with the last three fingers of the left hand. The right hand should then be placed on the club and pressure applied by only the second and third fingers. The only fingers applying pressure are: the last three fingers of the left hand and the middle fingers of the right hand. The remaining fingers play a supporting role, but you have to do something with them so, you want to adopt one of the three standard grips, the interlocking, overlapping, or the baseball hold. They are all designed for personal comfort according to the shape and size of your hands. Experiment to find

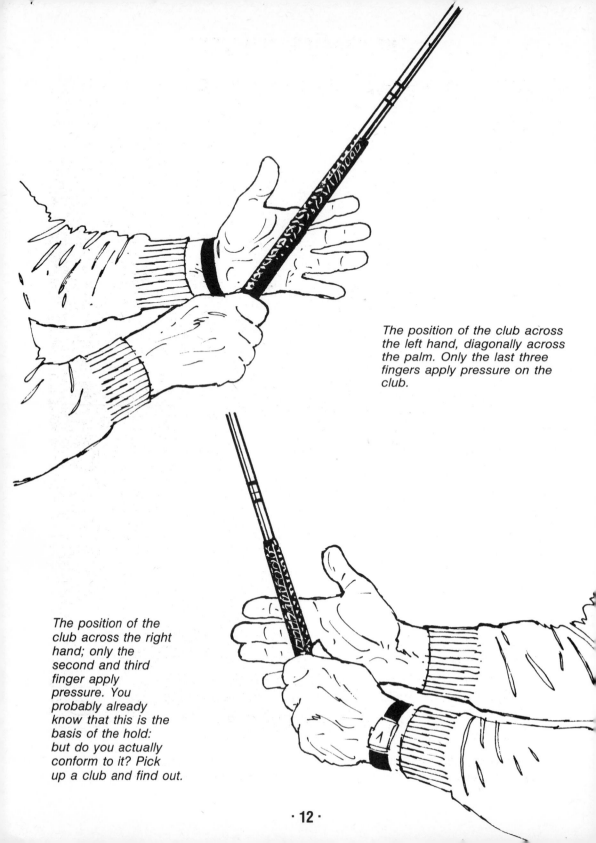

The position of the club across the left hand, diagonally across the palm. Only the last three fingers apply pressure on the club.

The position of the club across the right hand; only the second and third finger apply pressure. You probably already know that this is the basis of the hold: but do you actually conform to it? Pick up a club and find out.

The great Arnold Palmer at the 1970 British Open, St Andrews; you can actually see the looseness of the index finger of the left hand on the club.

GOLF

Seve Ballesteros chipping during the 1989 Ryder Cup; the 'V' formed by thumb and forefinger of each hand pointing mid-way between face and right shoulder.

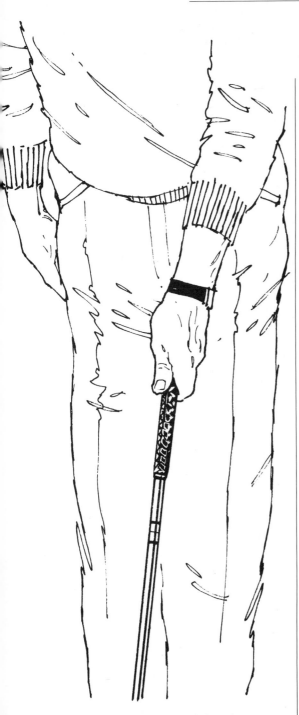

The club as held by the left hand.

out which one best suits you. Whichever hold you adopt, you must make sure both hands are as close to each other as possible, and that the hands and club work together as one unit.

When placing your hands on the handle of the club the little finger of your left hand should be approximately 1in (2.5cm) from the butt end of the club. This is a general rule, not a hard and fast one. If you are having severe difficulties then move your hold further down the handle

It is very important that the club grip lies diagonally across the palm of the left hand. This helps to create the correct angle of the left wrist. To enable the right hand to hang in the correct position the club grip must lie across the middle joints of the fingers. This ensures that both palms are facing each other. Note how the grip on the club tapers downwards to help us to place the fingers of the right hand.

If you now place the club head on the floor, with the club correctly lined up between ball and target, the 'V' formed by each of your thumbs and index fingers should both be pointing to a mid-way point between your face and right shoulder. No matter what club you use or which hold you adopt, the 'V' should always point in the same direction.

Most players wear a glove on their left hand; this is a personal choice. It is worn to prevent the club slipping from either a wet (caused by perspiration), or dry hand. Don't forget, a very dry hand is also a slippery hand. The glove will improve the hold on the club but, perhaps more important it makes you more aware of your left hand. The left hand is very important: you must maintain your correct hold throughout the shot.

Now for one of those often confusing areas, keeping the left arm straight. The novice is constantly, and rightly, told to keep his left arm straight. But he often gets confused and thinks the left arm and

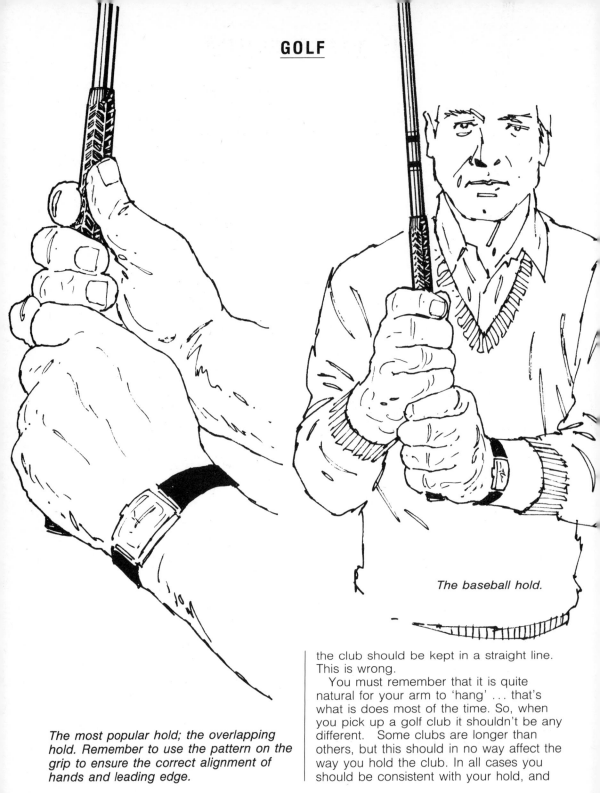

The baseball hold.

The most popular hold; the overlapping hold. Remember to use the pattern on the grip to ensure the correct alignment of hands and leading edge.

the club should be kept in a straight line. This is wrong.

You must remember that it is quite natural for your arm to 'hang' ... that's what is does most of the time. So, when you pick up a golf club it shouldn't be any different. Some clubs are longer than others, but this should in no way affect the way you hold the club. In all cases you should be consistent with your hold, and

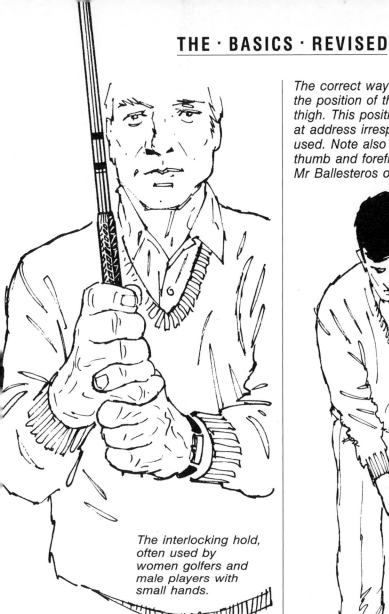

The interlocking hold,
often used by
women golfers and
male players with
small hands.

The correct way to hold the club. Note the position of the hands in relation to the thigh. This position should be maintained at address irrespective of which club is used. Note also the 'V' formed by the thumb and forefinger, as demonstrated by Mr Ballesteros on p.14.

should always make sure your hands marry up with the leading edge. If you look at the grip on your club you will see a pattern. Use it to line up your hands and club with the leading edge. The pattern is a visual aid to your hold and if the club is held correctly then the part of pattern you are using as your aid should be central on the handle.

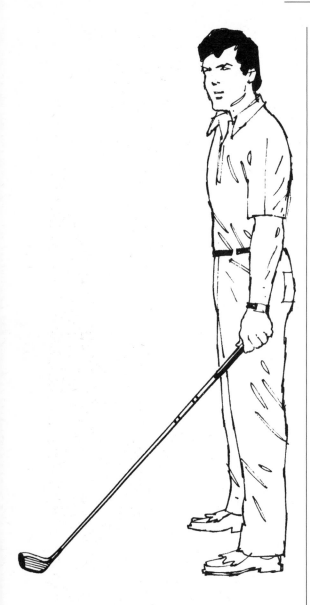

This is the natural way to hold a golf club, thus dispelling the myth that the left arm should be straight at all times. If you held your arm by your side and then inserted a club into your open hand, this is the position both arm and club would assume. This is similar to the correct position for both at address.

. . . And not *with the left arm completely straight and as an extension of the club.*

Hale Irwin displays the perfect follow-through. Note how his elbows are kept together and how the toes of his right foot are supporting him.

A square *club-head at address.*   *An* open *club-head at address.*

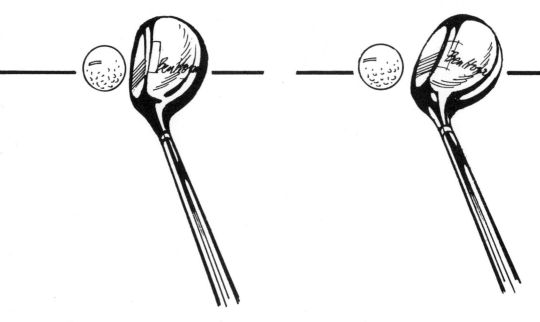

THE · ADDRESS

The are two basic address positions; with the ball in line with the heel of the left foot; and with the ball positioned between the two feet. The former is used for shots with wooden clubs and longer irons and, as the club selection moves to the medium and short irons, so the address position moves to the point between your feet. When in the address position, no matter where the ball is in relation to your feet, your left hand should cover an area over the inside of your left thigh.

The best rule for knowing where to stand in relation to the ball is to line the club-head up square to the ball and in the direction of the shot. Then adopt your stance, making sure your hold is correct and that your hands are in line with the leading edge. Your right foot should then be square to the ball-to-target line and your left foot will automatically adopt a position about 15 degrees to the left of the ball-to-target line. The back of the heels, however, will be parallel to the ball-to-target line.

You'll soon be getting fed up of hearing this term leading edge but we cannot emphasise it enough. The leading edge is more important than even the face of the club because, if you get the leading edge in the right place at the right time then the face will hit its target. There are numerous shapes of swings but there is only one correct contact and in one direction.

When lining the ball up with the target area you will often see the better players stand behind the ball first. This is not only to see where they are aiming but also to pick out a landmark, *i.e.* some natural feature about 3–4ft (1m) away that will assist in creating a line of ball-to-target. The ball will then be lined up with the landmark rather than with the target and the body set absolutely parallel to the ball-to-target line.

THE · BASICS · REVISED

A closed *club-head* at address.

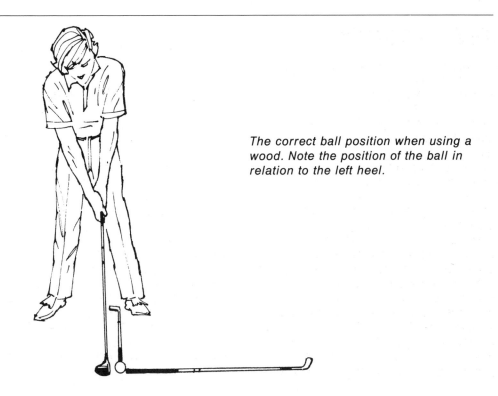

The correct ball position when using a wood. Note the position of the ball in relation to the left heel.

This time see how the ball has moved further away from the left heel as the club gets shorter.

Ball-to-target line

The normal stance at address. It is often referred to as the square stance.

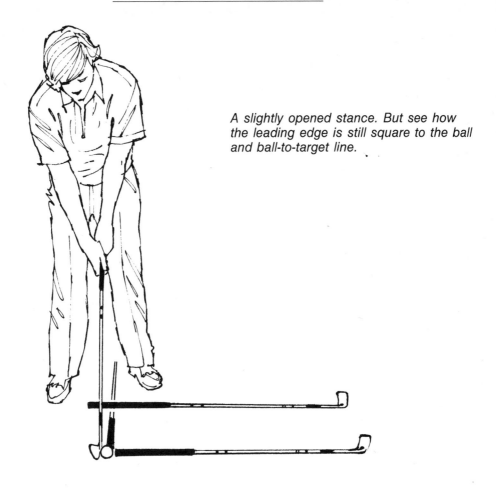

A slightly opened stance. But see how the leading edge is still square to the ball and ball-to-target line.

BODY · POSITION

Your body position is also an important part of the golf swing. You don't, as many people believe, have to line your body up with the swing. But you do have to line the ball and club up with it. If you are using a wood, you should bring your right foot back slightly from the line of direction. This is because the wooden club is longer than the irons and you need to get your right shoulder out of the way when executing the swing. A slightly closed stance when playing a wooden club should be encouraged because it enables a good pivot.

Alternatively, if you are playing a short iron then you can adopt an open stance to enable you to get your body through and towards the target. Because of the nature of the swing you aren't going to have time to get your body through. An open stance will allow you to do this.

Posture is very important. Many novices tend to bend their knees to adopt a near-seated position. This does not allow the

GOLF

The correct alignment of the ball with the target.

flexibility required to effect a good swing.

To achieve correct posture, no matter what your sex or age, you should stand upright, and then bend the back slightly forward. The hips and rear-end will stick out. This may look unnatural, but you have now adopted your correct angle of spine which is crucial and must be maintained throughout the full swing. This position creates the tilt of the golf swing and enables the shoulders to make a good 90-degree turn while the head remains steady and the hips rotate at a

45-degree angle. Now you should gently flex the knees towards each other. Each knee, in turn, plays an important role in the swing.

When you have adopted this posture and lined your club up, you will find that your right shoulder is slightly lower than your left and your head is slightly behind

Britain's Laura Davies has awesome power and has shown in recent years that she is a match for the top Americans.

GOLF

At the top of the backswing and the completion of the turn of the upper body, your left shoulder should be pointing at the ball.

Note the head position at address – slightly behind the ball. Note also how the knees are flexed and in the 'ready' position.

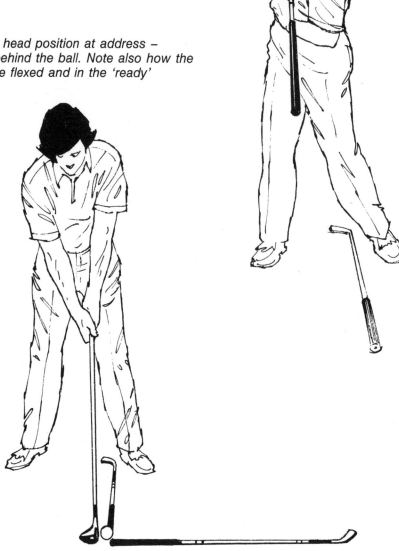

the ball. It must not be over the ball otherwise it means you are stretching forward and even before you have started your swing your balance is out of place.

Make sure your body is square to the ball-to-target line and that the inside of your right arm is pointing outwards so that if you removed the club from your hand you could bring the hand straight up to touch your shoulder. Your weight distribution will change from being equal on each foot to slightly more on the left and then the right foot. This will be discussed later in the book.

The width of your stance depends on the type of club being used, and, of course, your own physical make-up. But as a guideline, for woods and long irons your feet should be a shoulder width apart with the width measured to the inside of the shoes. For short iron shots the feet should again be a shoulder width apart, but this time the distance is measured to the outside of the shoes. You should bend your knees slightly towards each other, so they are in a 'position of activity'.

You will often see players 'waggle' their clubs before lining up a shot. The 'waggle' is no different from the tennis player bouncing the ball several times before serving. It enables them to get a feel of the length and weight of the club, the pressure of the hold, and it can also be a means of relieving tension. Many players don't even realize they are doing it. Some shuffle their feet instead of, or as well as, waggling the club.

So far, we have got to understand the club, sorted out the aim, got the hold right and adopted a comfortable posture ... all highlighting that golf is a game of movement. Now it is time to put all these together and get the swing into action to see if it all works properly.

THE · SWING

The first, and probably most important, part of the swing is the takeaway, that part of the backswing when the club is taken from the ball to a waist-high position.

The takeaway is a movement whereby the whole left side – the arm, leg, shoulder, hip, shaft and club – moves towards the right side. The takeaway occurs because the right hip and shoulder move back slightly. The hands and wrists maintain their shape in relation to the shoulders. Consequently the arms stay the same distance apart as when they set out at the address position, and the pressure of hold as exerted at address is maintained.

It is important to remember that the face of the club does not have to be square to the target at all times during the backswing. Therefore, as soon as you start the takeaway, don't worry about the club face no longer being square to the ball. Remember how the club face appears to open as it stays square to the moving body.

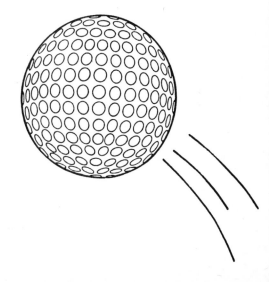

GOLF

The 'Blue Print' golf swing from the address to the follow through.

The left arm, position of legs and head position should be noted during each aspect of the swing.

GOLF

After the takeaway, continue the **backswing** in a continuous movement of the upper part of the body as the club is raised up by the hands and arms. Keep your eyes firmly fixed at the back of the ball and observe the following important points:

(a) Allow the wrists to 'cock' naturally.
(b) Make sure the pressure on the hold is maintained.
(c) Keep the left arm comfortably straight.
(d) When the club is at the top of the backswing the elbow of the right arm should point at the ground just behind your right heel.
(e) The shaft of the club should, at the top of the backswing, be pointing parallel to the ball-to-target line.
(f) Make sure the elbows at the top of the backswing are the same distance apart as they were at the address position.

Now you have got to the top of the backswing, next comes the most crucial part of the entire swing, the first 1½–2in (4–5cm) of the downswing. This is the last point of the swing when you can sensibly think about what you are doing; after that it is down to the club and gravity. Once you have gone beyond those couple of inches you have to go ahead confidently with the swing.

At the top of the back swing, the club should be parallel to the ball-to-target line with the club-head pointing at the target.

Nick Faldo looks satisfied with this long-iron shot in the autumn sunshine
during the World Matchplay Championship Final at Wentworth, 1989.

Make sure everything comes down together, just as it did going up, and don't forget that more of the face of the club will be visible at the top of the swing and less will be visible as you bring it back to the ball for the final lining up of the leading edge before contact.

The action of the downswing sees the hips carried through slightly ahead of the hands as most of your weight is transferred to your left leg by the movement of the hips, enabling the top half of the body to remain square at impact. This is all made possible by maintaining a steady head and consistent spinal angle.

As you follow though your head remains steady, which makes the hip action rotational, until such time as the pull of the club-head causes your head to be pulled up and and you can take your first look to see where your ball has gone. You will now be facing the target with your weight on your left leg, your right leg bent at the knee, and your right foot completely on the toe of the shoe.

If you have followed those guidelines you should have no problems hitting the golf ball accurately. However, it is

The top of the backswing from behind. See how the elbow of the right arm is pointing towards the ground by the right heel, and how the elbows are the same distance apart as they were in the address position.

Lanny Wadkins at the Belfry; perfectly balanced, the hips have rotated, the head has come up with the pull of the club-head, the right knee is bent, the left foot turning over.

GOLF

inevitable that you will encounter problems from time to time. If you do, come back to this chapter, because it is a good bet you are performing one of the basics incorrectly. Is your hold still sound? Are you aligning the ball correctly? Are you adopting the wrong posture? These are just some of the problems which arise

without the player knowing it. But the slightest error can have an adverse effect on his or her game. You should never feel that your game has somehow gone beyond the basics of the swing; if Nick Faldo is prepared to review and adjust his swing, then so should you.

A simple and effective way of warming up while you are standing on the first tee waiting to play. It loosens up those muscles required in the golf swing.

WARMING · UP

It is worth considering doing some limbering up exercises before a round of golf. A footballer wouldn't go into a game cold. The golfer is no different. The exercises will loosen up your muscles, and help develop your swing. Try the following

before each round.

(a) Hold your hands out in front of you, in the 'shake hands' position. Put them together and swing from side to side but keeping your left arm straight and your head in a central position in the backswing, and your right arm straight in the follow through. This is nice and simple

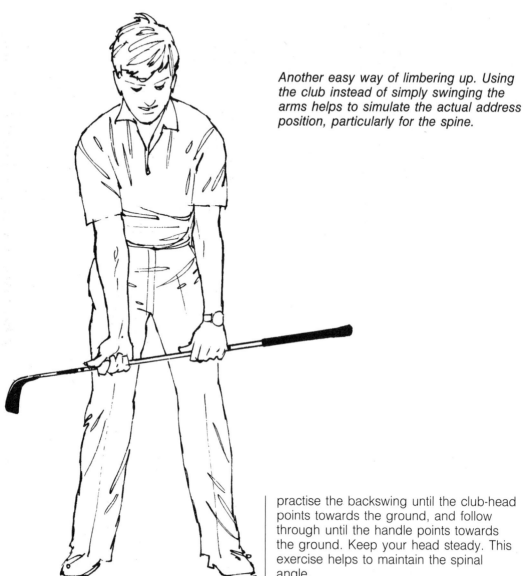

Another easy way of limbering up. Using the club instead of simply swinging the arms helps to simulate the actual address position, particularly for the spine.

practise the backswing until the club-head points towards the ground, and follow through until the handle points towards the ground. Keep your head steady. This exercise helps to maintain the spinal angle.

(c) Hold the club across your back, supporting it with the tops of your arms. Pivot to the right, as if taking up the backswing, until the club-head points to the ground, then pivot to the left until the handle points to the ground, keeping your head steady.

(d) Finally, to help make you more aware of the backswing and follow

and forms the basis of the golf swing.

(b) Hold a club in front of you with the club-head to the left, your left hand over the shaft and right hand under it, and thumbs pointing away from the head. Keep the arms a shoulder width apart and assume the address position. Then

THE · BASICS · REVISED

through, take hold of three clubs simultaneously and swing them with your normal swing.

The swing is an important part of golf but, you should never forget that there is only one correct contact and one direction. All the advice above is open to your own interpretation. Seve Ballesteros has a different swing to Nick Faldo, Larry Nelson has a different swing to Jack Nicklaus. But they all have a blue-print to work to. We have given you that blue-print. Go away and practice and develop your own style.

And another way to loosen up those muscles before a round of golf.

... Once more, this is the form of a simulated swing.

Mark Calcavecchia surprised a few people when he won the 1989 British Open, but he has been displaying his skills and talent on the US tour since 1981.

TWO

THE

TEE SHOT

The tee shot can be played with any club from a driver (No.1 wood) through to a wedge but, of course, you wouldn't play the wedge off the tee at a 465-yard (423m) par 4 hole! We are going to concentrate on playing the tee shot with the longest club in your bag, the driver.

When teeing the ball up, make sure that at least half of the ball is showing above the top of the club-head.

Because the face of the driver has very little loft, playing with it requires the very best of swings. The near-flat face of the club-head makes contact with more of the ball, so there is a greater risk of imparting side spins, which can lead to the dreaded slice or hook. You should by now have a better understanding of your swing, and should not encounter too many problems with your No.1 wood off the tee.

The first thing to learn is how high to tee up the ball. The simple rule is: high enough to have at least half of the ball showing above the top of the club-head. This rule would apply if you were driving with a 3- or 5-wood but, of course, because the face of these woods is not as deep as the driver, the ball would, in effect, be teed up lower.

Having teed up your ball, you now have to adopt the correct stance. Your body position and posture will be the same as for the standard stance as outlined in the opening chapter. The ball should be positioned level with a point approximately 1–2in (2.5–5cm) from your left heel. To see this more clearly determine your ball-to-target line and place a club in the direction of the target. Place another club at right angles to the ball and adopt your

American Paul Azinger shows the follow-through of a tall thin man.

stance. You will then get a clear picture of where your left heel is in relation to the ball.

Because of the position of the ball in relation to your body, your head will be positioned behind the ball. Don't be tempted to bring your head forward and in line with the ball.

When adopting your stance, your right foot should be slightly drawn back from the ball-to-target line, as was explained in the previous chapter. So your weight will be slightly transferred to your right leg. Bringing the foot back will give the feeling of your weight being shifted to it anyway.

It is important on the backswing that you get a full 90-degree shoulder turn. It is also crucial at the top of the backswing that the club is parallel to the ball-to-target line. It does not have to be horizontal, but it must be parallel to the ball-to-target area. There is nothing to stop the club-head becoming horizontal, but you should avoid it going beyond the line of the horizontal.

The important thing to remember, and something that we will keep emphasizing no matter which shot you are playing, is the need to keep the shape of the club throughout the swing. Do that, and most of your problems will be solved.

Talking of problems, most faults appear, and are created, before the moving swing starts. So, if you are having problems driving, look, at your stance, hold, etc.

You will see many of the leading professionals using long irons off the tee these days. This is because they can achieve great distances with irons and are reducing the risk of error, while maintaining distance. There is nothing wrong with using an iron off the tee, and if you do, everything is the same as for the driver except you don't need to tee the ball up so high, and the ball gradually moves away from the left heel to a midway point between the two feet as the club gets shorter.

Many problems with the No.1 wood occur due to overswinging, because it is the longest club in your bag. The length of the backswing is determined by the need to maintain your hold on the club and keep well balanced.

THREE

FAIRWAY WOODS

The object of the game of golf is to get the ball from the tee into the hole in the least number of strokes. The best way of getting from the teeing area to the putting surface is simply by hitting each shot as far as possible; hence the need to play wooden clubs off the fairway. But, as you are well aware, not all fairway shots are with woods.

You wouldn't play a wood to a green 60 yards (54m) away, but you might consider using a wood with, say, 160 yards (145m) to go. But, again, local conditions, the weather, and the lie of the ball are all factors in the choice. Once you have decided that you are going to play a wooden club off the fairway, it requires a good shot to get the distance and accuracy required.

Wooden clubs range from No.1 (the driver) to No.5, although it is possible to get 6 and 7 woods. However, the recognized set of woods these days is 1, 3 and 5. The face of each wooden club, like the irons, is angled. The greater the club number, the greater the angle of club face.

We have already dealt with the driver. The first thing you will notice about the other woods is how the face is shallower than that of the No.1 wood. Because of this you are able to play woods off the fairway. Playing the driver off the fairway is left only to the best of players. Don't attempt it at this stage of your development.

The length of the handle on the woods gets shorter as the club number increases but the length of the grip is the same for all wooden clubs.

GOLF

While all woods will give you more distance than irons, the 3-wood will give more than the 5-wood, and so on. But, if your lie is tight and your stance less than level, it is advisable to choose the 5 rather than the 3, and it may be better to select an iron rather than a wood at all. Only you can decide that, when the situation arises.

Your stance and swing with a fairway wood is the same as for the basic swing. The ball should be slightly away from the left heel, but not in a central position between your feet. It is important to make sure your club-head is allowed to sit completely on the ground. If you look at the club-face you will see an insert. This is a useful aid to enable you to see the bottom of the club-face at address. It also helps you to line up the club-head with the ball. A common fault with many high-handicap players is the failure to place the club-head correctly on the ground. Many think the top of the club-head is the leading edge when it is really the bottom of the face.

Once you have positioned your club-head correctly, the remainder is the same as the swing for the driver. Don't forget, make sure the shape of the club is maintained.

Curtis Strange was the biggest money winner in golf in the 1980s.

FOUR

LONG, MEDIUM & SHORT

IRONS

Every golf club is different in length of shaft and, of course, the angle of loft on the club face. It is when you come to using your irons that these differences will be fully appreciated because the range of loft varies greatly from the 1-iron to the pitching or sand wedge.

The long irons are those numbered 1–2–3–4, and the first thing you must appreciate when using them is that as the club number increases, so the shaft becomes more upright when the club-head is placed on the ground. Consequently, each club has to be played differently. You cannot adopt the same stance for a 1-iron as for a 9-iron.

Long iron play falls into the realm of the 'long club' category (like the woods). Therefore you will play these irons with your longest swing. Stance and swing are the same as the 'blue-print'. The ball position for a 1-iron is approximately the same as for a 5-wood. It moves progressively towards a central position between your feet as the club number increases.

Your shoulders should be level with the inside of your heels; as when playing wooden shots. The right-foot should be drawn back slightly from the ball-to-target line. As we showed you in the opening chapter, this enables your body to get in a full swing.

When playing with medium irons (5, 6 and 7), you should stand closer to the ball and your shoulders should be level with the outside of your heels. Feet, shoulders, knees and hips should now be square to the ball-to-target line and your weight evenly distributed between both legs.

A full swing is not necessary when playing a medium iron, and the stance is more upright. Consequently, the swing becomes shorter.

Because the ball is now positioned nearer the mid-way mark between your feet, your head is not as far behind the ball as with the longer clubs. It is still, nevertheless, behind the ball. Don't be tempted to put the head level with, or ahead of, the ball.

The swing will now be more upright, so divots will appear after your club strikes the ball. They are a result of the ball position and the angle at which the club-head makes contact with it. Don't forget to replace all divots.

Finally, the short irons are the 8 and 9 irons, and the two wedges; the sand wedge and pitching wedge. All three have a short swing but can be used for a full shot as well as for the short approach shot around the green.

Don't be afraid to play the wedge off the fairway for those 80–90 yard (74–83m) approach shots – it is not just for playing delicate chips around the green and out

The correct stance for an iron shot.

of the bunker.

At the address position, the ball should be mid-way between your feet, and your left foot should be drawn back slightly from the ball-to-target line with your weight transferred slightly onto it. The feet and hips move back, not the shoulders. This is because the swing is short and less body movement is required. Therefore you need to have your left side out of the way to enable your trunk to come through to complete the stroke.

As we have quickly come through the clubs from the driver to the wedge, you will have appreciated that because of the club design, the ball position in relation to your feet has altered from a point level with your left heel to one level with the middle of your feet. As the clubs have got shorter, your feet have moved closer together. But if you take up a stance with your driver and then with a sand wedge you will note one very important common factor: your left hand is still covering that area of your left leg just above the knee. If it's not, then you've got to go back to basics.

All clubs are different, and stance changes with them. So does the swing. It becomes more upright with the shorter irons. But, no matter which club you are playing, you must always maintain the shape of the club. How often have you heard playing partners say their driving was great today but their medium iron was awful? That is because they were trying to play a 6-iron the same way as a 3-wood. You can't. Each club is different. Remember: long clubs gave a long swing; medium clubs have a medium swing; and short clubs have a short swing, all governed by the length and lie of the club.

FIVE

FAULTS

& THEIR CORRECTION

Before looking at the common faults that will creep into your game from time to time, it is worth understanding what is meant by swing path and ball flight.

SWING · PATH

If you look at the diagram you will see that the correct position for your feet, is within the ball-to-target line. The area on the other side of that line is known as the outside.

To play a normal straight shot, your club should be swung from inside, hit the ball, and follow through on the inside of the ball-to-target line. This is known as the inside-to-square swing.

A swing that goes over the ball-to-target line, striking the ball, and following through on the inside is called an out-to-in swing. Conversely, the swing that starts on the inside, hits the ball, and then continues its travel on the outside of the ball-to-flight line is known as the in-to-out swing.

We will outline the effect of each of these later when we start analyzing faults, like the slice and the hook.

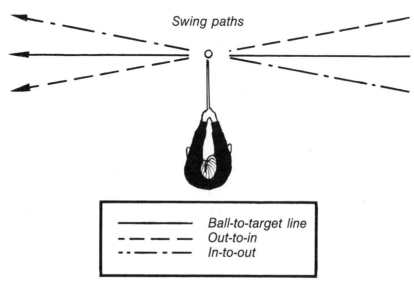

Swing paths

	Ball-to-target line
	Out-to-in
	In-to-out

BALL · FLIGHT

There are several flights the ball can take. The most common are: the straight flight, the hook and slice, (which are common faults among many players), and the pull and push, (again, faults which often creep into the high-handicap player's game). But both the pull and push can often be used to good effect by the more experienced players, who will also have the deliberate hook and slice in their repertoire.

There are two other common flight paths; the draw and the fade. The draw is a deliberate shot, created as a result of a slight in-to-out swing path with the face of

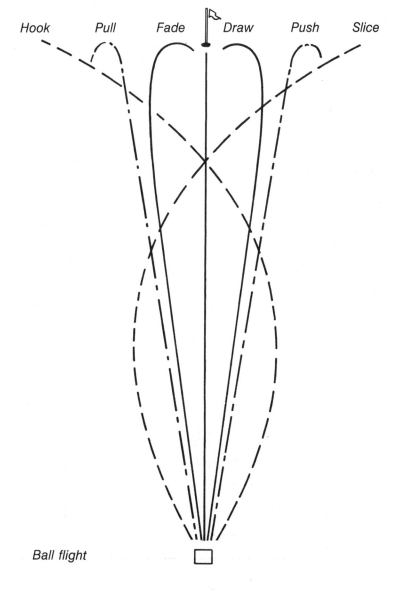

Hook   Pull   Fade   Draw   Push   Slice

Ball flight

the club square to the ball-to-target line at impact. The ball starts its flight slightly right and the square club-face brings it back towards its target. Good players will use the draw as a way of gaining maximum controlled distance.

The fade is also deliberate, and is created by adopting a slight out-to-in swing path, again with the face of the club square to the ball-to-target line at impact. This time the ball starts slightly to the left of the target and, because the club-face is square at impact, comes back towards the target.

It is now possible to look at faults that could develop in your game and discover ways to correct the mistakes.

SLICING

Along with the hook, the slice is the scourge of many players. So what causes the slice? Well, there are a lot of possible causes, the following are the major reasons:

(a) The club-face is open at address. Consequently, the leading edge is open and, as we have emphasized, the leading edge must always be square to the ball and ball-to-target line.

(b) One or both hands are too far to the left around the grip. This is called a weak hold.

(c) The ball is positioned too far forward at address. As a result the shoulder line is open.

(d) Rolling the club-face open at the start of the backswing. The address may be fine, but the moment the takeaway and backswing starts, the club-face is

A most popular visitor to British shores is American Ben Crenshaw.

In this example, the elbows have become too far apart and the right elbow is far too high. The club will be across the target line at the top of the backswing.

opened. The likely outcome is a slice. The answer lies in maintaining the shape of the club in relation to your body.

(e) The club is taken away on the outside: as a result an out-to-in swing path can be created. The shoulders will not be fully turned at the top of the backswing and the club will be laid-off, *i.e.* pointing to the left of the target. So make sure the takeaway is a one-piece movement.

(f) Overswinging because the hands have lost their grip on the club is another possible cause of the slice, as there will not be enough pressure on

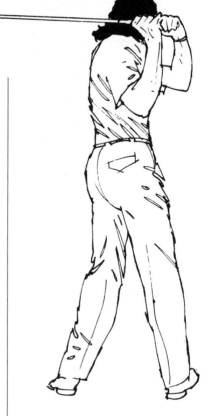

the club at the address. The result will be a separation of the arms, commonly known as a flying right elbow.

(g) Starting the downswing with the shoulders, as opposed to the legs, hips, hands and arms, is another likely cause of the slice.

(h) A collapsing left arm at contact will certainly do no shot any good, and will probably result in a slice.

With this list of likely causes, it is little wonder that many players, even the world's best, occasionally slice a ball. But, if you are slicing regularly, you only need to look through the list and you will find one (or more!) reasons why you are slicing. Rectifying the problem is easy: just go back to basics.

A common feature among players who slice with woods and long irons is that they will very often miss the target to the left when playing medium and short irons, because they pull with an out-to-in swing with the club-face square to the ball-to-target line. The result will be a pull.

This time, the right elbow is too close to the player's side because the left arm is too bent.

One of the causes of the hook – the club going across the target line.

HOOKING

Now for the possible causes of the hook:

(a) The biggest cause of hooking is having the club-face closed at address. In other words, the leading edge is turned inwards.

(b) One or both hands are too far to the right on the handle. This is known as a strong hold.

(c) The ball is positioned too far back at address, which results in the shoulder line being closed.

(d) Closing the club-face by moving the hands too far forward at address.

(e) The club at the top of the backswing has gone across the target line and is pointing to the right of the target.

(f) The right elbow and upper arm are held too close to the body in the back- and downswing.

If you are hooking work through this list of possible causes from a to f.

TOPPING

Getting the ball airborne is often a problem to the newcomer. The tendency is to 'lift' the ball off the ground, but that is not necessary: the angle of loft on the club-face will do that for you. Provided your swing and swing path are correct, the club-head will get the ball airborne. However, if you are occasionally topping, then look at the following probable causes.

(a) Ball too far forward at address.
(b) Ball too far away from your feet.
(c) Your bodyweight is shifting to your left leg on the backswing and to your right on the downswing, resulting in your body coming up at impact. This is often incorrectly called 'head up'. The head does come up but it is not as a result of any head action. It comes up automatically because of the bad shifting of bodyweight.
(d) Head position too low at address, with your chin too close to your chest. This also causes your body to come up at contact.
(e) A collapsing left-arm at the top of the backswing. It doesn't straighten in time to make a good contact.
(f) Pressure of hold too tight, causing tension on the backswing, which will cause a lifting of the body.
(g) Ball teed too low.

Unlike topping, the thin shot will move the ball forward, whereas a topped ball will hardly go forward. The thin shot occurs when the ball is hit in the middle rather than on the top (when 'topping'), or on the bottom with a good shot.

FLUFFING

Hitting the ground before the ball is known as fluffing. It is the result of too steep an attack on the golf ball, brought about by a steep downswing. And the probable causes of this embarrassing event are twofold:

(a) Ball too far back at address, causing the shoulders to tilt, the arms to go too high in the air, and too much weight to be transferred to your left leg during the backswing.
(b) The club travels further than the body has turned. The result is a stab down on the ball on the downswing.

Hooking, slicing, topping and fluffing are all relevant to swing planes and swing paths. An understanding of swing paths will help eliminate these often infuriating aspects of your game. Keep the sequence of the 'blue-print' swing in mind at all times and it will help you to build a good golf swing. A good swing always reduces the risk of error.

Following hot on the heels of Ballesteros is another great Spanish talent, Jose-Maria Olazabal.

SIX

SLOPING LIES

Sloping lies fall into four distinct categories: uphill lies, downhill lies, ball below the feet, and ball above the feet. They are not easy to play, particularly the latter three. But if you follow these procedures then you shouldn't encounter too many problems.

UPHILL · LIE

1. The first thing you must do is endeavour to make your frame perpendicular to the slope.
2. Because you are playing uphill, the trajectory of the slope will automatically cause the ball to get airborne. As a result you want to take a stronger, less-lofted club, than the shot dictates. As a guideline, if you are playing off a severe slope (as shown in the example) you want to take a club two less than normal. If it is a mild slope then take one club less.
3. Having set your body perpendicular to the slope, keep you head position steady which will ensure the club-head swings down and up the slope.
4. The ball should be slightly back from its normal address position and a slight in-to-out swing path should be

When playing the uphill lie make sure your body is perpendicular to the slope, and keep your head steady.

SLOPING · LIES

A good extension of the arms through impact from Mark James.

employed, causing a tendency to hook, so aim slightly to the right.

DOWNHILL · LIE

1. This is an extremely difficult stroke to play and it is important that you hold your body perpendicular to the slope throughout the swing. The tendency is for the head and body to move forwards.

2. If the slope is severe, as in the example shown, select a club more lofted by two club lengths. If the downhill slope is not as severe it should be greater by one length.
3. The ball position should be slightly back in the address and aimed slightly left of the target. The reason for this is the tendency to create a slight out-to-in swing path.
4. Allow the natural curve of the ground to create the swing path.

The same rules apply to the downhill lie. The body should be perpendicular to the slope and the head steady. There can be a tendency for heads to move forward – beware of this.

When playing a ball below your feet, flex your knees slightly more than normal and use the full length of the club handle, holding it near the top of the handle.

BALL · BELOW · THE · FEET

1. Use the full length of the handle of your golf club and grip it near the top of the handle.
2. Flex the knees slightly more than normal to stop your weight falling too severely towards the ball.
3. Position the ball midway between your feet.
4. Aim slightly to the left of the target.
5. During your downswing your weight is likely to fall forwards to the front of your feet, and this is likely to create an out-to-in swing path. However, if you aim the ball slightly left in the first place you will see the ball travel from the left towards the ball-to-target line.

BALL · ABOVE · THE · FEET

1. The ball position should be midway between your feet.

2. Aim slightly to the right of the target.

3. Shorten your hold on the handle to allow for the elevation of the ground and the slope.

4. Because of the lie of the land you will be taking a flat swing which will cause the in-to-out swing path, resulting in the controlled hook. That is why the ball is aimed slightly to the right in the first place.

There is one important word to remember when playing any of these four shots: ambition. Don't be too ambitious with your expectations. The uphill lie will be the easiest of the four shots to play, but the other three require the very best of techniques. What you must do is consider where your next shot is going to be played from. Leave the fancy stuff to the professionals.

When playing a shot with the ball above your feet, you must shorten the handle by holding the club further down it.

SEVEN

GETTING OUT OF
TROUBLE

We ended the last chapter by telling you not to be too ambitious when playing shots from sloping lies. Let's be frank. If you find your ball in trouble it is because **you** have made a mistake. Who is to say you aren't going to make another mistake while trying to get out of trouble? Most high handicap players make the fatal mistake of believing they can play a shot out of the rough in exactly the same way as they play a fairway shot. Don't fall into that trap.

Analyze your **next** shot and decide on the course of action which will make it easier. If you have to stab the ball out of the rough a few feet and onto the fairway, then do it; it is worth sacrificing a shot to get into the right position for your next shot. There are many times when you will find yourself getting into bigger trouble by playing the ambitious shot from a difficult position. So, don't be too ambitious with your recovery. Here is some guidance on playing out of two trouble spots.

Getting out of long rough requires a lofted club played with an upright swing.

LONG · UNCUT · GRASS

The big danger with this shot is that the grass will wrap itself around the shaft of your club, resulting in a closed club-head at contact. The following points will help you:

1. Take a club heavy enough, and with sufficient loft (sand iron), to allow for the wrapping of grass around the shaft. The heavier the club, the more chance it will still make its way through the grass and to the ball.
2. You want to adopt a steep angle of attack on the ball rather than sweeping the club through the long grass. To get the steep angle, adopt a more upright backswing. At the moment of contact there will still be loft on the club.
3. Reiterating what we said earlier … don't be too ambitious.

If your ball is in the light rough don't forget it will probably be 'sitting up'. You must therefore shorten your club by holding it further down the handle.

CUT · ROUGH

This is the apron between the fairway and the uncut rough. It is designed to penalize you if you play into it, but not as severely as the uncut rough, when a lost ball can well be the outcome.

The big problem with playing out of light rough is believing that your ball is sitting up and that you have a good lie. The ball will be sitting up high because the grass is longer than on the fairway, and if you adopt your normal swing your club-head would travel under the ball, and the golf ball would go into the air. So, consider the following points:

1. Shorten the hold on the handle. Move your hands further down the handle in order to make the club shorter.
2. Create a firmer hold on the club.

In addition to landing in the rough there will be other occasions when you find yourself in trouble and most of your other problems will come in the form of sand. We will be covering bunker play in greater detail later in the book.

No matter what kind of trouble you are in, don't forget that you have already made the mistake by being in trouble. Ease up on your expectations as a result of playing out of trouble. If you can make one mistake, you can easily make two.

EIGHT

PITCHING & CHIPPING

Pitching and chipping are known as the 'short game', and it is essential that you develop a sound knowledge of the skills pertaining this aspect of the game.

PITCHING

The pitch is played with a lofted club designed to hit the ball into the air with less than a full swing. The following are key points when playing pitch shots:

1. The leading edge of the club should be at least square, if not slightly open, to the ball-to-target line.
2. The golf ball should be positioned just left of centre at address and your feet should be slightly opened to the ball-to-target line.
3. Adopt your normal hold.
4. Keep your shoulders square to the ball-to-target line.
5. Take slightly more of your weight on your left leg than normal. During the backswing you need to make sure that your weight is not shifted and it remains on the left leg. However, as the downswing commences with your hands, arms and club, more weight moves onto the left leg.
6. To regulate distance move your hands further down the handle for the shorter shots and higher up the handle for longer pitch shots.
7. The follow-through should be at least the same length as the backswing.

Pitch.

Tom Watson shows how the hands stay ahead of the clubhead when chipping.

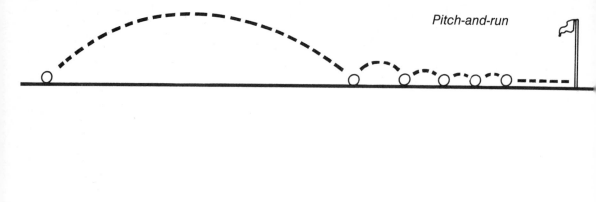

Pitch-and-run

Chip.

Pitching is a 'hand and arm' shot. You don't need to rotate your hips and body. However, it is important that the face of the club should appear to grow to the onlooker as it is taken into the backswing. We covered this in detail in the opening chapter, but it comes back to what we have said many times: The shape of the club must be maintained, no matter which shot you are playing. Remember, a pitch is a lofted shot, so take a lofted club, and keep the loft on the club.

If you have to pitch a ball lying on hard ground, take your most lofted club and position the ball slightly back from where it would be for a conventional chip.

Remember to resist the temptation to scoop the ball to gain height. The loft on the club will do this for you. And also resist the temptation to curtail the follow through.

CHIPPING

The chip shot is played with a medium iron, and pitches the ball into the air slightly before running on to its target. Key points to remember when chipping are:

1. Hold the club further down the handle.
2. Take the loft off the club by holding your hands slightly forward at address. This is known as hooding. Despite taking the loft off the club the leading edge must remain square to the ball-to-target line.
3. The bodyweight distribution and stance is similar to that for the small pitch, *i.e.* the bodyweight is slightly on the left leg and the feet are slightly open to the ball-to-target line.
4. Don't cock your wrists, and move your hands, arms and club together. This will help keep the club-head lower to the ground. The club-face will not

appear to get as large to the onlooker as we have seen with many other shots.

The chip is also a 'hand and arm' shot and they must be kept forward of the ball at contact. This action creates the 'chip and run'. When playing a chip, or chip and run, you should aim at the hole. When playing a pitch you should aim at the flag. By aiming the chip at the hole you allow the ball an area to run into. By aiming the pitch at the flag, you are making provision for the loft of the shot to drop into, or near to the hole.

Don't expect the ball to stop every time you pitch to the green. Much depends on the texture of the area from where you play the ball and, of course, the texture of the green. You won't get a ball to stop dead on a rock hard green in the middle of summer . . . so don't expect it to!

The professionals are able to create a lot of backspin on the ball, as they achieve superb blade contacts on the ball. You can not expect to be able to do this every time you play a pitch, and backspin can only be regularly created when the putting surface is soft enough.

Remember that when you are pitching to a green below your stance and ball position, the ball is more likely to stop on pitching than if the green and putting surface is well above the ball and your stance.

When to chip and when to pitch are decisions which you will regularly face during a round of golf. We cannot give

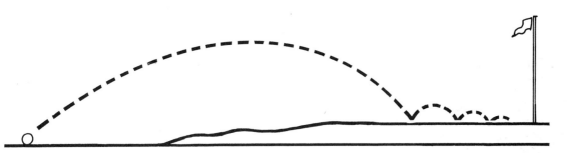

Pitching to a green above your stance and ball position.

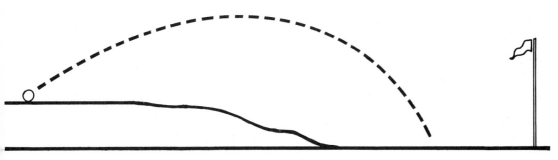

Pitching to a green below your stance and ball position.

you the answer; local conditions and the lie of the ball will dictate such action – even weather conditions will play an important part in your decision.

There is no sense in trying to pitch a ball that is lying on rock hard ground, whereas lush grass will lend itself ideally to the pitch. Wind, and texture of the ground, are also important factors to consider when deciding upon the chip or pitch. Finally, don't be frightened to use your sand iron for pitching.

To maintain the high standard of the putting surface presented to us by the groundstaff, it is essential that you carry a pitch repair fork, and develop the habit of repairing pitch marks on the putting green every time.

NINE

PLAYING OUT OF
BUNKERS

Bunkers are strategically placed around the golf course to catch wayward or badly played shots. There are two types of sand bunker, the greenside bunker, and the fairway bunker. Both often have other names when you land in them, however!

Most novice golfers are petrified of landing in a bunker, or rather, of trying to get out of a bunker. But the following tips will help you to play successful shots out of sand.

As we have said earlier, practice is the only way to perfect any aspect of your game, and this cannot be emphasized more than with bunker play. You are most probably thinking; 'Well, if I've done everything right in the first place I shouldn't need to worry about playing out of bunkers.' That is true, but you only have to watch the world's top golfers to know that even the best of them land in bunkers at some time. Remember Greg Norman's plight in the play-off for the 1989 British Open at Troon?

Gary Player is one of the finest bunker players. He spent hours pitching balls from a bunker onto the putting surface to achieve his skills. It is that dedication that makes you a better player. With the confidence that comes from that kind of repeated exercise, the bunker shot can be aggressive, rather than a damage limitation shot.

Now for some tips on how to play bunker shots. First, we will look at the greenside bunkers, and assume that the ball is lying on soft sand in the bottom of the bunker.

1. Before going into the bunker, have a look at your shot from behind the ball towards the flag and from the side to assess the distance of the shot. Enter the bunker with the least sand disturbance, feeling the sand texture with your feet. Don't pick up the sand to feel it, that is not allowed. And don't forget, you are not allowed to ground your club in the bunker. The first time your club-head makes contact with the sand is during the play of the stroke.
2. You should adopt your normal grip with the face of the club open.
3. Aim the leading edge towards the ball-to-target line, again remembering the club-head cannot touch the sand.
4. Adopt an open stance, with your shoulders, hips, knees, and feet aimed to the left of the target. When taking up your stance, wriggle your feet into the sand to get them comfortable. If the sand is very soft your feet will be slightly below the ball, and you will have to shorten the handle by moving your hands slightly down the grip.
5. The ball should be positioned towards your left heel.

Playing the bunker shot. Even though the stance is open the leading edge of the club is still square to the ball and ball-to-target line. Because of the open stance, note that the 'divot' taken by the club-head is parallel to the line of stance.

6. Fix your eyes on the sand at a point approximately 2in (5cm) behind the ball.
7. Make a wrist and arm backswing along the line of your shoulders.
8. Swing your hands, arms and club down and through the sand, continuing along the line of your shoulders, ensuring all the time that the face of the golf club continues to look at the ball-to-target line through impact. The club-head initially strikes that area 2in (5cm) behind the ball and the open club-face lifts the ball out of the sand. The shot is played by bouncing the back of the sole of the club on the sand.
9. Your head position must be kept steady throughout the swing, and it is advisable to create a full follow through.
10. The distance your ball has to travel, and the texture of the sand, will decide how much sand you hit. For less distance you would take, say 3-4in (10cm), and maybe only 1in (2.5cm) if you require more distance.

Not all bunker shots are that simple. For example, the ball may be plugged. If it is, take note of the following:

1. Adopt your normal grip but this time have the club-face closed. That may sound strange at first, but the swing is played so violently that action at impact will open it.
2. A square stance should be adopted with the ball in a central position between your feet.
3. The stroke is again played by taking sand first and it should be played with a violent downswing. Because the ball is plugged you know the sand is soft. Therefore it is possible to play the shot with violent downswing without risk of injury.
4. Try to create a follow through.

GOLF

Note how Mark McNulty has set his body position for the slight uphill bunker shot.

GOLF

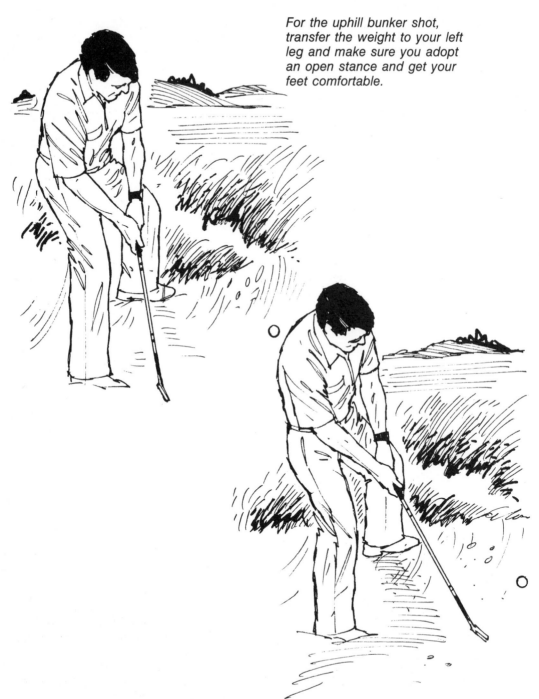

For the uphill bunker shot, transfer the weight to your left leg and make sure you adopt an open stance and get your feet comfortable.

... The shape of the club must be maintained throughout the shot.

5. The ball coming out of the bunker is inclined to run on after hitting the putting surface, so try and allow for this.

Now for balls that are on the up slope of the bunker.

The biggest problem here is catching the lip of the bunker with the ball as it is exiting the hazard. To overcome this you want to set an open, and well-balanced stance. Because you will be standing with one leg higher than the other, you will need to transfer some of your weight to your left leg to create an address which will allow the club-head to swing down and up the slope while maintaining the loft on the club face. Have a look at what we told you about playing uphill lies. This shot is similar.

Next follows advice on playing the ball when it has come to rest in the back of the bunker, I'll bet you're now beginning to wish bunkers didn't exist!

The big problem with this shot is deciding whether you stand in or out of the bunker. No matter where you have to take up your stance, you have to create a more severe upright backswing and

The awkward bunker shot – the one at the back of the hazard. Getting a good stance is often the problem but it must be an open stance. To avoid the club-head making contact with the back of the bunker an upright swing has to be adopted.

downswing, to avoid hitting the lip of the bunker both going back and coming down. By adopting this upright backswing you will create a very open club-face. Balance and follow through are two essential points in this shot.

Having looked at getting out of greenside bunkers there are also the fairway bunkers to consider.

Where the ball finishes in the bunker determines what you can try to achieve. Remember, when we discussed getting out of trouble earlier in the book, we said you must always consider your next shot. If it is likely to be more beneficial to play the ball out of the bunker a few yards on to the fairway then do it. Don't take a 1-iron and expect to hit a ball pin-high on to the green from a bunker 170 yards (155m) away. Leave those shots until you become more expert.

Until you gain experience caution is the correct attitude to adopt when playing out of fairway bunkers and you should not attempt a club more powerful than a 7-iron.

A normal grip is adopted when playing out of fairway bunkers. Your stance should be square and the ball should be positioned slightly left of centre. Make sure you have a firm left-hand grip. This time you should focus your eyes on the top of the ball, not the sand behind it.

We mentioned earlier that you should take care when entering the bunker and ensure the minimum amount of sand disturbance. If you leave footprints around the bunker, you could find your ball in one of them if you don't get out of the hazard first time.

It is your responsibility to make sure the bunker is clean and tidy after you have been in it. So make sure you rake it after exiting and whatever you do, you must not exit the bunker from the front.

That's bunker play. There is a lot to remember when you step into that bunker but if you have followed these guidelines then you should not be in the bunker too long. We used the word ambition when talking about getting out of trouble. Remember that word when you are faced with a bunker shot.

Severiano Ballesteros shows how to keep the loft on the face of the club when making a bunker shot.

TEN

PUTTING

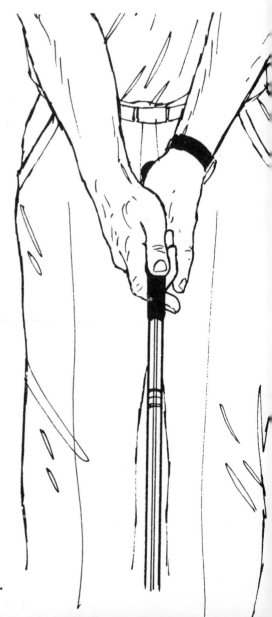

Now for that area of the golf game where many holes, matches and tournaments have been won and lost ... the putting surface. It is here that you can destroy all your good work on the tee and fairway with a poor putting technique, and the inability to 'read' greens. It can also offer a chance to salvage something from poor approach play.

You should aim to take no more than two strokes once on the putting surface. Any more can be regarded as failure. Long putts, of course, make life that little bit harder, but you should draw a mental picture of the golf hole and imagine it to have a diameter of 6ft (2m). Aim to get the ball into that area. If you do then your next putt will be no more than 3ft (1m).

The following guidelines will help towards improving your putting technique.

1. The ball should be lined up square with the club-face and in line with the centre of it.
2. The club-face should be at right angles to the ground and square to the point of aim

The putting hold is different to the normal hold. Nine of your ten fingers make contact with the club handle and both thumbs are placed on the flattened part of the handle. The index finger of your left hand is the only one that doesn't make contact with the club. The index finger of your right hand can be wrapped around the club handle.

PUTTING

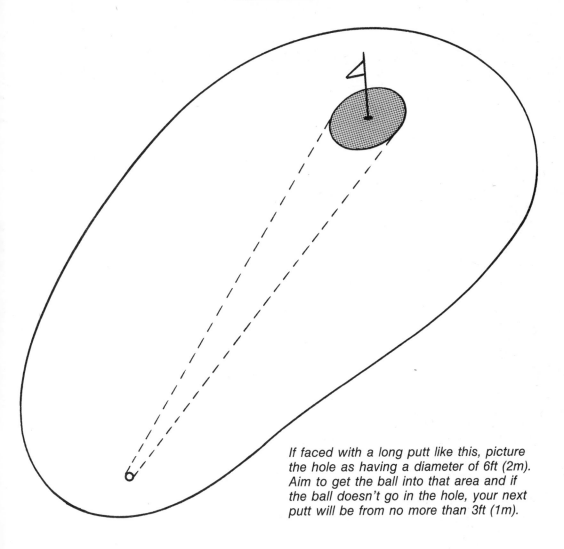

If faced with a long putt like this, picture the hole as having a diameter of 6ft (2m). Aim to get the ball into that area and if the ball doesn't go in the hole, your next putt will be from no more than 3ft (1m).

3. The hold of the club is most important, and the most popular is the reverse overlap. With this grip, seven of your eight fingers, and your two thumbs, actually hold the club handle. Consequently, you have a more secure hold of the club, which helps to maintain an accurate movement of the putter.
To effect the overlap grip, place the four fingers of your right hand on the grip and your thumb on the flattened part of the handle. Most putters have flattened handles on one side to enable you to get both thumbs on this part of the grip. The last three fingers of the left hand also grip the handle and the thumb again rests on the flat part of the handle. The index finger of the left hand runs across the fingers of the right hand (as seen in the diagram), or it can be placed down the grip

PUTTING

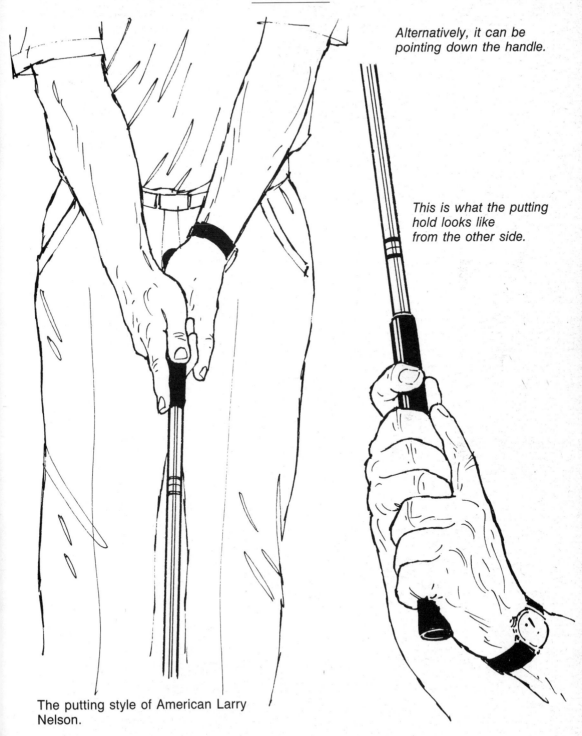

Alternatively, it can be pointing down the handle.

This is what the putting hold looks like from the other side.

The putting style of American Larry Nelson.

When putting, ensure that your head is directly over the ball.

The reason we hold the club in this way with the thumbs down the front of the handle and with the left index finger outside the hold is to try and eliminate the cocking of the wrists. The putting stroke is a movement of the arms, shoulders, and club only, and you should spend quite a bit of time practising it because it is so different from the normal golf stroke The putter should be an extension of the arms, not the hands, and pressure on the club should be with authority, but not too tight. And remember; always give yourself enough backswing to make a forward stroke.

4. The ball position at address can vary according to each player's style but the most common is opposite your left foot. The ball at this position encourages a top spin strike.
5. The width of stance again varies, but the most common is with the outside of your shoes level with your shoulders.
6. Posture is important when putting. You want to bend at the waist to make sure

PUTTING

The hands should be in front of the ball.

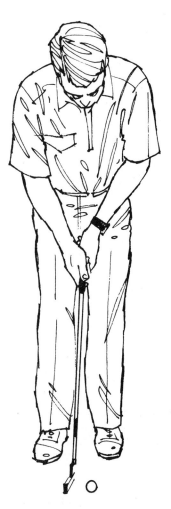

your head and eyes are directly over the ball at address. Your bodyweight should be evenly distributed or slightly on to the left leg. During the making of the shot your body position and head position must remain still. Balance, posture, and weight distribution are of great importance when putting.

These guidelines assume everything is nice and simple and you have a straight putt. However, putts come in varying distances, and you are advised to practice short, medium and long straight putts.

They should not be behind it.

GOLF

As you take the club back, note how only the arms move.

The putting stroke does not require a complete body movement or shoulder rotation.

Having trained yourself to hit the ball in a straight line you are ready to consider the 'borrow' on the greens.

Putting surfaces, while magnificently manicured by greenkeepers, are not flat level surfaces like billiard tables. They contain ridges, borrows, and other individual peculiarities. You must be able to 'read' the green in order to determine your putt.

Tom Kite putting ... note how his hands, arms and club all move as one unit.

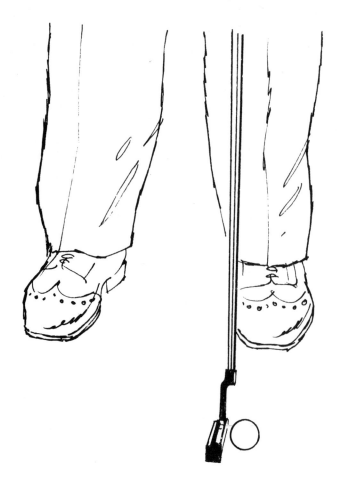

Note the position of the ball in relation to the feet when putting.

Reading borrows of the green is very important. But assessing the speed of the putt is equally important because speed determines borrows. The slower the putt the more any borrow will be accentuated, and vice versa.

The correct way to assess a borrow on a green is to look from behind the ball towards the hole. The best way to test the speed is to walk the length of the putt, but not on the line of the putt, and observe the ground from a side angle. You will see leading players assessing the lie of the putt from every conceivable angle, but they have had years of experience of reading greens and know exactly what they are looking for. Furthermore, they often have a few thousand pounds riding on single putts. There is no need for you to spend that much time on reading your putt and often the old adage that your first decision is the right decision should be followed.

You were advised to practise short, medium, and long straight putts earlier. The reason for this is simple: all putts are straight putts. Perhaps you are now

PUTTING

Don't *cock the wrists when playing the putting stroke.*

PUTTING

confused, but the explanation is simple. All putts are straight, it is the borrow which makes them appear otherwise. If you read a borrow 6in (15cm) to the left, you play your stroke 6in (15cm) to the left and let the borrow bring the ball into the hole.

Putting is an acquired skill improved through years of practice on different greens. There is no mystique to putting, just practice and experience.

Quite often you see putts up to 10ft (3m) missed, and the main reason for this is that at address you can see the hole out of the corner of your eye and the tendency is to look at the hole as you are putting. There is a golden rule when putting: hit and hark. In other words, head steady, play the stroke, and wait to hear that great sound of the ball dropping into the hole.

Finally, when should you have the flagstick in the hole, when do you have it removed? If your ball is on the putting surface the flag must be removed. If your ball hits the flag from a putting stroke on the green, it is a penalty. You can have the flag tended by a playing partner, or caddie, but it must be removed after the stroke has been made.

However, if your ball is off the putting surface you have the option of leaving the flag in the hole, having it tended, or removed. In all cases there is no hard and fast rule.

When you have reached the putting surface, have consideration where you will be exiting the green when making for the next tee, and leave your equipment at that side of the green near to your exit point. It improves the speed of play and shows consideration for those players behind you. Whatever you do, you must never take your trolley onto the putting surface, and you must not place your golf bag on the green.

Note how Spaniard Jose-Maria Olazabal has his head over the ball when putting.

ELEVEN

FACING THE
ELEMENTS

Rain and wind are the two worst weather conditions you will find yourself playing in. Anything more severe than that, like snow and ice, and your local course will probably be closed anyway.

One aspect of playing in wind and rain that many golfers ignore is the chill factor. If you are cold, no matter what you are trying to do, your performance is affected. If the weather is bad, make sure you are suitably dressed to keep warm.

PLAYING · IN · WIND

If there is anything likely to destroy a good golf swing it is a very strong wind. It may seem to be a nice day when you set out on your round of golf but by the time you get into the middle of the course and into those unprotected areas, there can be winds swirling around all over the place.

The golden rule with strong winds is never take on the wind, you won't beat it! In other words, don't look at a shot with a strong wind against you and think, 'I reached it with a three iron last week, so I should do it again this week.' You must allow for the wind, and take a club that is stronger. You are not taking on the wind, but are allowing for its strength.

Because of the wind your swing could be thrown off balance. To help you make a more well-balanced swing you should move your hands down the grip by 1–2ins (2–5cm). If the wind is so severe that it is likely to blow you completely off balance you should decrease the amount of action of your feet and legs.

If the wind is blowing from behind downwind, make use of the wind because it will allow the ball to fly further: you are going play with the wind.

Take a more lofted club than the shot would normally require. This way you will get the ball airborne quicker than normal and will get more distance. Care, however, must be taken when playing lofted clubs downwind. You could see your ball go through the green.

Probably the worst type of wind (for a right-handed golfer) is the left to right wind, because it is at your back and will almost certainly blow you off balance. Furthermore, the flight of the ball is going to move considerably from left to right. To allow for this you must aim to the left, according to the strength of the wind. You must then make sure the ball is hit straight, so the wind brings the ball back towards the target.

The right to left wind is similar to its left

Mark James enjoyed his best ever season in 1989 and was a regular and consistent performer on the European PGA Tour.

to right counterpart but this time of course your aim should be to the right to allow the wind, again, to bring the ball back towards the target. (Just because we said the left to right wind is probably the hardest of all shots to play in adverse conditions, don't believe that the right to left is easy ... it certainly isn't).

We have talked about strong headwinds, downwinds and crosswinds, and in all cases have assumed the ground and lie of the ball to be level. But there will be times when you will have to play a sloping lie with a crosswind. Provided you clearly understand the basic golf swing, and make adaptations for these particular shots, then you shouldn't encounter too many problems.

PLAYING · IN · RAIN

If you play most of your golf in Britain then I'm afraid you will find playing in the rain a fairly regular occurrence, so you may as well be prepared for it.

Rain means cold. And this comes back to what we said earlier about the chill factor. It is important to wear the correct clothing when playing in rain, and that includes a hat. Included among your equipment must always be a towel for keeping your hands, gloved or otherwise, and grip, dry. Once your grip becomes sodden it is extremely difficult to control.

It is possible to buy gloves especially made for playing in wet conditions. These all-weather gloves are made of a fabric or material capable of absorbing the moisture or water collected on the grip. You can also have the grips of your clubs changed so they are full or half cord grips. Again, these will help to absorb the water.

An umbrella is a must when playing in rain as it helps to protect you and your clubs from the elements between shots.

Playing in rain is no different than playing on a normal day, except that you have to wear outer clothing. But you must always be prepared for rainy conditions. Make sure you know where your waterproofs are in your bag, and be able to get them on quickly. And don't forget, if you have items in your trouser pocket, like a pencil, scorecard, pitch fork, tees, or a ball marker, transfer them to your waterproofs before putting them over your normal clothing. It is frustrating for your partners and/or players behind you who have to stand and wait while you sort yourself out. So, preparation and thought are two key words when playing in rain.

Waterproofs are made of lightweight material these days, and do not hinder your golf swing. For advice on which waterproof suit is best for your own needs you should consult a PGA professional at a nearby golf course. He will advise you sensibly and offer you a wide choice of suits.

If you don't have waterproofs you should consider getting some as soon as possible. Don't, whatever you do, wear a top with a fitted hood. The hood will certainly restrict your movement and impair your view of the ball.

People who wear spectacles are at an obvious disadvantage when playing in the rain. They may gain some relief by wearing large peaked caps or visors but I'm sorry, its something you spectacle-wearers are going to have to live with.

Rainfall creates a slippery surface so you must therefore make sure your shoes are in good repair, and they are fully studded.

After incessant rain you will occasionally find, depending on the lie of the ball, that your feet sink into the turf at address. Consequently your feet are going to be below the level of the ball. To compensate for this you must shorten the length of your hold by moving your hands slightly down the grip.

And finally, don't forget that rain gathers on the golf ball and it is not until it gets airborne that it gets shaken off. You can, of course, wipe your ball dry once it is on the putting surface, but not while it is on the fairway. So you should consider taking a more lofted club than normal. For example, if you would normally take a 3-wood, then take a 5-wood, because the ball gets airborne quicker. The distance obtained will probably be very little different from that gained with the 3-wood.

OTHER · ADVERSE · CONDITIONS

Snow generally closes golf courses and while play can continue on frozen ground, courses are likely to offer temporary greens. Frost causes the inevitable problems of slipping during the swing. Overhitting is also a problem with frosty conditions because of the hard ground.

There are obvious dangers of playing in thunder and lightning and if it arrives you are well advised to stop playing and leave the course at once. Don't shelter under a tree and, unless you have a modern umbrella with built-in safety measures for such conditions, don't put it up.

The only other weather condition to mention is extreme heat but, again, if most of your golf is being played in Britain, it won't affect you too much! However, in the event of a heatwave, you should check local rules and conditions about dress. On no occasion should you enter a golf course without a shirt and in many cases the wearing of shorts is not allowed. Always check the required dress for the club you are playing at.

Before playing golf you should make sure you have all your equipment ready for all kinds of weather conditions and of course, you should check the weather forecast.

TWELVE

GOLF RULES

A FURTHER EXPLANATION

In *Play the Game* we covered most of the rules of golf but there are still some questions that may be unanswered. That is why books have been written on the subject of the rules of golf alone. We will now clear up one or two more important rules.

How long can be spent looking for a lost ball?

A ball is deemed to be lost if it is not found or identified as his by the player within five minutes after the player's side or his or their caddies have begun to look for it.

When can a provisional ball be played?

If a ball may be lost outside a water hazard or may be out of bounds, to save time the player may play another ball provisionally as near as possible to the spot from which the original ball was played.

The provisional ball should be played before the search for the original ball begins. If the original ball is found then it is the ball in play and the provisional ball should be lifted and not played. If not, then the provisional ball is played under the penalty of one stroke.

If a provisional ball is not played and the original ball is not found, then what happens?

If a ball is lost outside a water hazard or is out of bounds, the player shall play a ball, under penalty of one stroke, as nearly as possible at the spot from which the original ball was last played.

How do the rules differ for a ball lost in a water hazard?

A provisional ball can still be played if there is reason to believe the first ball will be in the hazard (as for out of bounds). If a provisional ball is not played, then, under a one stroke penalty, a second ball can be played from a position as near as possible to where the ball was last played. However, there is a second option, under a two stroke penalty, to drop a ball behind the water hazard, keeping the point at which the original ball last crossed the water hazard directly between the hole and the spot at which the ball is dropped, with no limit to how far behind the hazard the ball may be dropped.

Irishman Ronan Rafferty displaying the complete follow-through.

How do you know where the out of bounds areas are?

They are clearly indicated on the reverse of the scorecard which you collect from the professionals shop before the commencement of your round. Don't forget that any local rules, applicable only to the course you are playing, are to be found on the reverse of the scorecard as well. Make a note of them before you commence play.

If a ball is not lost, but is unplayable, what action must be taken?

The player may declare his ball unplayable at any place on the course except when the ball lies in or touches a water hazard. The player is the sole judge as to whether his ball is unplayable. If he deems it unplayable, he shall, under penalty of one stroke

(a) play his next stroke as nearly as possible at the spot from which the original ball was last played

or

(b) drop a ball within two club lengths of the spot where the ball lay, but not nearer the hole

or

(c) drop a ball behind the point where the ball lay, keeping that point directly between the hole and the spot on which the ball is dropped, with no limit to how far behind that point the ball may be dropped.

If an unplayable ball lies in a bunker and (b) or (c) are chosen then a ball must be dropped in the bunker.

What are the rules concerning casual water on the fairway, green and in bunkers?

First of all, casual water is described in the rules as: any temporary accumulation of water on the course which is visible before or after the player takes his stance and is not in a water hazard. Dew is not casual water.

Relief can be obtained from casual water if your ball is in or touching the casual water, or it interferes with your stance or intended swing.

If the casual water is on the fairway (through the green) then relief is obtained as follows: the point on the course nearest to where the ball lies shall be determined which is (a) not nearer the hole, (b) avoids interference by the conditions, and (c) is not in a hazard or on a putting green. The player shall lift the ball and drop it without penalty within one club length of the point thus determined on ground which fulfils conditions (a) (b) and (c)

If the casual water is in a hazard and the ball lies in or touches a hazard, the player shall lift and drop the ball either:

(a) without penalty, in the hazard, as near as possible to the spot where the ball lay, but not nearer the hole, on ground which affords maximum available relief from the condition

or

(b) Under penalty of one stroke, outside the hazard, keeping the point where the ball lay directly between the hole and the spot on which the ball is dropped.

However, if the ball is in a water hazard or lateral water hazard, relief cannot be obtained without penalty.

If the casual water lies on the putting green the player shall lift the ball and place it without penalty in the nearest position to where it lay which affords maximum available relief from the condition, but not nearer the hole nor in a hazard.

What is a lateral water hazard?

It is a water hazard, or that part of a water hazard, so situated that it is not possible, or is deemed impracticable by the Committee, to drop a ball behind the water hazard in accordance with the rules.

The part of a water hazard to be played as a lateral water hazard should be clearly marked and defined by red stakes or lines.

Relief from a ball lost in a lateral water hazard is by dropping the ball outside the water hazard within two club lengths of either (i) the point where the original ball last crossed the margin of the water hazard or (ii) at a point on the opposite margin of the water hazard equidistant from the hole. The ball must be dropped and come to rest not nearer the hole than the point where the original ball last crossed the margin of the water hazard. A penalty of one stroke is incurred.

Can the ball be teed up anywhere on the teeing area?

No, it can only be played from the teeing ground which is a rectangular piece of land, the front of which is defined by two tee markers. These also define the sides, and the teeing ground extends behind the markers by a distance of two club lengths.

What happens if a ball lands on the wrong green?

The ball must be moved to the point on the course nearest to where the ball lies provided it is not nearer the correct hole or is in a hazard or on the putting green. This mark shall be determined and the ball dropped within one club length of that point, at no penalty.

What happens if a ball is played out of turn?

In pairs matches, the rules are as follows. In match play, the opposing player can insist on the ball being replaced and the shot played in the correct order. In stroke play, however, no penalty is incurred and the ball is played as it lies.

In threesomes or foursomes (where both sides play one ball) the rules are different.

If a player plays when it was his partner's turn in a match play competition, then they shall lose the hole. However, if the same thing happens in a stroke play event, then the stroke shall be cancelled and a two stroke penalty be incurred.

And what happens if a wrong ball is played?

In match play the hole is lost, unless the player plays a stroke with a wrong ball in a hazard. In stroke play, again unless in a hazard, a penalty is incurred; this time it is two strokes.

Something that many novices are never quite sure about is 'honour'. What is it and what are the rules concerning it?

The side entitled to play first from the teeing ground is said to have the 'honour'.

The rules of golf are quite categoric on the order of play. In match play the person or side which wins a hole shall have the honour at the second and all subsequent teeing grounds. The honour at the first is decided by lot or toss of a coin, or some other method. If the person with the honour from the teeing ground wins or halves the hole then he shall retain the honour.

Once play is anywhere other than on the teeing ground, the ball furthest from the hole shall be played first. If two or more balls are equidistant, the ball to be played first shall be decided by lot. A ball can be on the putting surface yet further away from the hole than a ball on the fairway: the ball on the putting surface still plays first.

In Stroke play the competitor with the lowest score at a hole shall take the honour at the next teeing area. The player with the next lowest score is next, and so on. If two or more players have the same score at one hole then the same teeing order from the previous hole is maintained.

Power and determination ... two of Greg Norman's trade marks.

GOLF

One of the most infuriating sights on any golf course is seeing a queue of golfers caused because of slow play or general time-wasting looking for lost balls. What are the rules concerning these situations?

Unless special or local rules dictate otherwise, two-ball matches have preference over three- and four-ball matches and should be allowed through. A single player has no standing and should give way to a match of any kind.

Any match playing a whole round is entitled to pass a match playing a reduced round. However, in all cases, if a match loses more than one clear hole on the match in front of it, then it should invite the match following to pass. In the interest of all, players should play without delay.

This rule is one of the 'priority on the course' etiquette rules of golf, but is one where commonsense must be adopted. If a ball is lost, there is no sense in, say, all four members of a fourball going in search of it. That means players from all directions leaving their bags to look for the lost ball. It all takes time and causes backlogs. If your party is a slow one then you should have consideration for those behind you. The rules regarding standing are irrelevant in such cases, and should give way to the law of common sense. If it is apparent a ball will not be easily found the match behind should be called through and only then should you start your five minute searching period.

While on etiquette, the rules of golf clearly lay down rules concerning the subject and it is worth clarifying these. To become a better golfer you should not only be able to play the strokes we have already discussed, but you should adhere to the rules of etiquette.

Safety

Prior to making a stroke or practice swing, you should always make sure nobody is standing close to you and in a position to be hit by the club. Consideration should also be given as to where the ball is going to go, and if objects like stones, twigs etc may fly up after playing the stroke and cause harm.

Consideration for Other Players

(a) The player who has the honour should be allowed to play his tee shot before the other players have teed their ball(s).

(b) No one should move, talk or stand directly behind the ball or hole when a player is addressing the ball or making a stroke. And of course you should not employ ungentlemanly tactics like dropping a club or 'chinking' money, keys, or other obstacles in your pocket.

(c) No player should play until the other players in front are out of range.

(d) When the play at a hole is completed, players should immediately leave the putting green but, as we have already said, give some consideration to the direction you will be leaving the green when you first approach the green.

Holes in bunkers

Before leaving a bunker a player should carefully fill up and smooth over all holes and footprints made by him ... and of course any left by others who have been ignorant of the rules.

Damage to greens, flagsticks, bags, etc

Players and/or caddie(s) should ensure that, when putting down bags or flag sticks, the putting surface is not damaged and that the hole is not damaged by standing too close to it. The flagstick should be properly replaced in the hole before all players leave the putting green. Players should not lean on their putters on the putting surface, particularly when they bend down to pick the ball out of the hole.

Golf carts (trolleys)

Local notices regulating the movement of golf carts should be strictly observed, particularly in wet conditions, when carts are often banned from the course.

Replacing divots, repairing ball marks and damage by spikes

On the fairway (through the green) a player should make sure that any turf cut or displaced by him is replaced at once and pressed down. Again, if any inconsiderate golfer has failed to replace a divot, then please do so. Don't forget, you mustn't damage the course with practice swings. If you make a divot, replace it.

Ball pitch marks on the putting surface should be repaired carefully with a pitch fork. If every golfer repaired two pitch marks every time he went on to a putting surface then putting greens would be even better surfaces. Mind you, there are an awful lot of people whose ambition it still is to make a pitch mark on a green!

Damage to the putting green by golf shoe spikes should be repaired, but not until all players have completed putting at the hole.

Damage through practice swings

In taking practice swings, players should avoid causing damage to the course, particularly the tees, by removing divots. Those are the etiquette laws as per the laws of golf, but of course commonsense also plays an important role in etiquette.

When a player is teeing off, don't stand in front of, or behind him. The correct place is directly opposite him. That way you are safe, and out of his line of sight. Naturally, you should keep perfectly still and quiet when another player is playing any shot, and on the fairway, you should avoid walking in front of balls in play.

The modern game of golf is slow, so always play your role in trying to speed it up. Keep an eye on where your opponent's ball goes. There is no pleasure in winning a game as a result of somebody losing a ball. Golf is a friendly game, keep it like that.

THIRTEEN

BUYING & LOOKING AFTER

CLUBS

& BALLS

We have discussed most of your golfing equipment elsewhere in the book and, of course, to be buying this book you will have already gone through the first stage of your golfing tuition and will have a set, or at least a half-set, of clubs.

Now that you are progressing as a player and are considering buying better and/or more equipment, you should seek advice, particularly in relation to the lie of the club, flex of the shaft and size of the grip, which are all important.

We have told you to take advice from your PGA professional on the playing of the game, and it is to the same person who you should go for advice on equipment. The service the professional can offer after years of training includes advice on equipment, play, and repair of clubs.

You only have to look through the many golfing magazines to realize there are countless different makes of clubs and putters, and trolleys, balls, gloves, waterproofs etc.

You can only afford to buy within your budget but this is where your professional will help you. He may advise you to buy a good quality half-set of clubs rather than an inferior quality full set, for example. It depends on how much you can afford, and how seriously you are taking your future development.

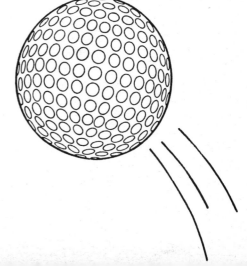

Gary Player taking a tremendous divot during the World Matchplay Championship at Wentworth, 1979.

It must be remembered when choosing clubs that a player's height affects the angle of the leading edge. That is why it is important to have the right set of clubs to match your physique. If not you will find the heel or toe of the club making contact with the ground when playing a stroke. If your clubs have forged heads then they can be bent to suit your needs. But don't try and do it yourself, take it to a specialist.

Looking after your golf clubs is a necessity if you are to play your best golf. Make sure the grips of the clubs are kept clean and that the grooves on all your clubs are cleaned out regularly. Dirty grips affect your hold on the club, while a dirty club-face affects the flight of the ball and can cause damage to the golf ball.

When it comes to selecting balls the only advice is; buy the best quality balls you can afford. When buying items of clothing like gloves, shoes, and waterproofs, you should make sure they fit properly and, do the job.

Ian Woosnam's follow-through is a fine example of how the back of the club-head becomes visible to the onlooker after completing its swing.

FOURTEEN

FITNESS
FOR GOLF

Golf in itself is good exercise. But don't be fooled into thinking that because you play golf you are keeping yourself fit. Like any form of exercise you must be fit before you take part. Golf is no difference.

It has been proved that once you have got yourself fit in the first place, it is a lot easier to maintain that level of fitness. Before we look into fitness in further detail it is worth outlining what happens to you if you are *not* fit.

The first thing you will notice is that physical tiredness sets in. And what happens if that gets a grip of you? First, your technique falls apart. Second, your sense of judgement fails. And third, decisions become increasingly hard, to make. You may blame your technique for a bad shot, but, stop and think – it may be the lack of fitness which brought about the bad shot.

So, right from the outset you can see how important fitness is. Get yourself fit and it will help you to enjoy the game more. It will also make you a better player.

How do you get fit for golf? Well, let's look at the demands this great game puts on you.

The physical demands stem from the technique of striking the golf ball. Each player develops his or her own specific swing or rhythm. But the physical demands of swing and timing are the same for every golfer.

In addition to this, there are the mental demands. Golf can be a very frustrating game and good mental concentration is called for. Golf can give you frustration, anxiety, worry, stress and elation ... all in one hole! So you can imagine how much pressure the mind is under for 18 holes.

The mental ability to cope with the weather conditions plays an important part. Many golfers don't like playing in the rain. Suddenly they start playing badly just because they have to put on their waterproofs. That is not because their technique has suddenly disappeared. It is because of a mental barrier.

There are two other demands that are put on the golfer. First, there is the demand imposed by expectations. Everybody, no matter what level they play at, has expections, about their own performance. And other people have expectations about your game as well. Golf is a great leveller in situations like these. Playing well is what all golfers strive for. Winning trophies is the next progression. The elation of winning a tournament cannot be described: you have to win one to find out what pleasure it brings. But once you have got used to winning, there comes the day when you lose. You may be able to go and hide yourself away in a corner somewhere. But

FITNESS · FOR · GOLF

Shoulder stretch.

Triceps stretch.

Wrist stretch.

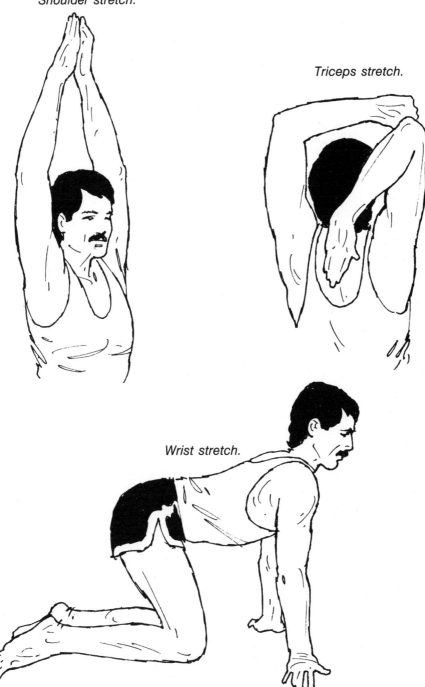

Side stretch.

Hamstring stretch.

what about the pressure put on you by the demands of other people who expected you to win? These are the environmental demands you will have to learn to cope with.

The major test for the golfer is of his or her own determination.
Golf is one of the finest games for testing your character. You cannot change the way you are, but your personality can certainly change once you get that club in your hand and stand on the first tee. To be successful you must have the determination to win and be able to motivate yourself to want to play. If you don't you will never progress beyond the level of an average club golfer. Golf has a horrible habit of kicking you in the teeth. You will need character to overcome these knocks.

Right. So these are the demands that golf puts on you. If you feel you can cope with them then let's carry on and get into the realms of fitness that will play their part in helping you to overcome each of those demands.

The inner game reveals itself; Seve's decisive chip to the final green at Royal Lytham to clinch the 1988 British Open.

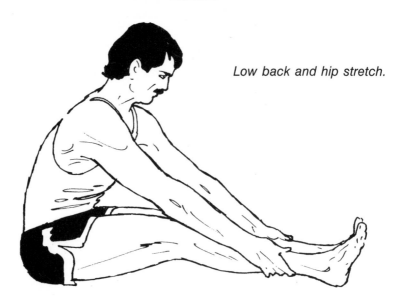

Low back and hip stretch.

THE · PRINCIPLES · OF
TRAINING

Whatever form of training you adopt must challenge your present physical stature and condition. This is known as the overload principle. If you have any doubts as to whether these exercises will do you any harm then you must seek advice from your doctor before carrying them out.

It is no good doing a bit of training for, say a week, and then thinking your are fit. The functional capacity of the body will return to what it was before the exercise. This is known as the principle of reversibility.

All forms of training must be specific and related to the game of golf. Don't go out and buy yourself a set of dumbells and do 20 pull-ups a day and think you're doing a good job. Your fitness schedule must be worked out to meet the demands of golf. Your training progress must be tested and measured, and compared with your level of fitness prior to starting your programme.

Before we look in detail at exercises, it is worth looking at what we are going to train for.

There is the mobility exercise which will help improve suppleness and improve the range of movements in joints. Golf puts a lot of pressure on your joints. Being fit will help keep them moving fluently, and also cut down the risk of injury.

We are also going to look at endurance training. Running is the best way to develop this. Once you have gone through this programme you will find that fatigue, often the curse of the golfer, will be considerably delayed. Speed training also forms part of golf fitness, but is game related. We don't expect you to be able to run like an Olympic sprinter, that's not necessary in golf. But speed is golf-related in its own way.

Strength training is another aspect of golf fitness but, as you are not likely to be entering the Mr Universe competition, you won't be lifting any heavy weights.

And finally the last reason for golf fitness training is to develop your skill, and the exercises will deal with practice of techniques.

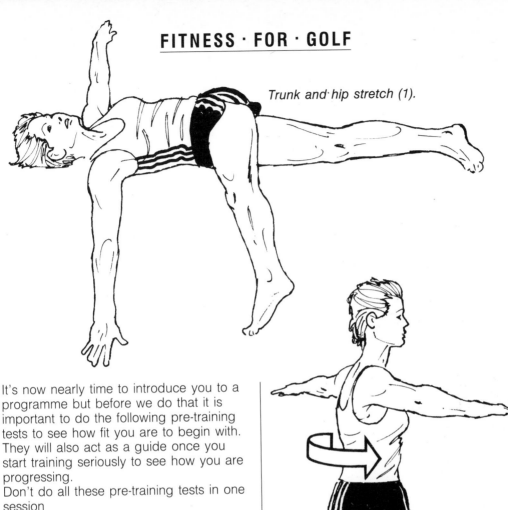

Trunk and hip stretch (1).

It's now nearly time to introduce you to a programme but before we do that it is important to do the following pre-training tests to see how fit you are to begin with. They will also act as a guide once you start training seriously to see how you are progressing.

Don't do all these pre-training tests in one session

Test 1: Either running, walking or jogging, see how far you can go in 12 minutes. It is best to take a road course so that you can then measure the distance in a car.

Test 2: See how far you can jump from a standing jump. Stand behind a line, keep you feet together and swinging your arms, jump away from the line. Measure the distance from the line to the landing point of your heel.

Test 3: See how far you can reach. Sit on the floor with legs apart and straight. With the arms straight together, see how far you can reach out on to the floor between your legs. Measure the distance from the crotch to the end of the outstretched fingers.

Test 4: See how far you can stretch. Lay

Trunk and hip stretch (2).

on your stomach and put your hands behind your back. Lift your chin off the floor and get somebody to measure the distance from the floor to the chin.

Test 5: See how far you can spring. Place two markers on the ground 10 yards (9m) apart and spring between them. Every time you touch one marker award yourself one point. See how many points you can score in 30 seconds.

Test 6: See how many press-ups you can do without pausing ... and no cheating!

Test 7: See how many sit-ups you can do. Lay on your back with your hands behind your head and legs straight. Sit up to an upright position and then down again. Count how many you do without pausing.

Test 8: See how many golf swings you can take. For one minute continuously swing a driver from the normal stance position; return to the stance position after each swing. Count how many you do in one minute.

Test 9: See how many single-handed swings you can take. Do as in the last test, but this time hold the club in one hand (left if you are right-handed, or vice versa),

Test 10: See how long you can lift your golf bag. Hold your arm straight and lift the bag up sideways away from the body to shoulder height. Time yourself first with the right hand and then the left hand.

Right, that's the pre-training tests over with. You will now have made a note of your 'score' on each discipline. If you've cheated then you've only cheated yourself and remember one golden rule of fitness training: no pain, no gain.

You are now ready to start a training programme. The programme should be carried out during the winter months and you should allocate sufficient time for it. There is no sense in rushing your exercises.

The build-up to serious training should be gradual. Take it steady for the first three or four weeks. After that you should be ready to progress and increase your output.

The following is an ideal programme, which is similar to the pre-training test. Some of the exercises in the pre-training test have been left out but you can always include them if you want to.

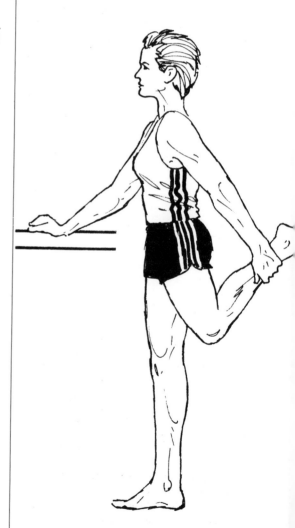

Quadriceps stretch.

First, go for a run four times a week. Aim for two miles at a time but don't worry if you have to stop for a breather to begin with. However, try and get back to running as soon as possible. Gradually build up the distance you run. If you can get up to five miles per session that would be ideal. You don't need to do any more than that, unless you are aiming to become a marathon runner as well as a good golfer.

You should also do some fast running four times a week. Lay out a marker at whatever distance you feel is ideal. Spring to one marker and then walk back to the other. Then spring again. Repeat this 12 times. Gradually increase the distance between the markers. But keep the number of sprints at 12.

Carry out the following body exercises four times a week:

(a) Sit-ups: take your pre-training test score and double it. For example if you did 20 on the pre-training you will now have to do 40, but not all in one go (see below).
(b) Press-ups: number as for sit-ups.
(c) Hop step and jump: this wasn't in the pre-training tests, so what you have to do is: Hop – from right foot to right foot; step – from right foot to left foot; jump – from left foot to land on both feet. The purpose of the hop, step and jump is to get as much height as possible.

Carry out the above three disciplines (a), (b) and (c) as follows:
- Do a quarter of your total sit-ups (which would be 10 in the above example)
- Take a one minute break, but keep moving around
- Do a quarter of your total press-ups
- Take a one minute break
- Do three hop, step and jumps,

Calf stretch.

starting from right foot
- Take a one minute break.

Repeat all the above THREE more times. With the hop, step and jump, alternate the start from the left and right foot.

Practise golf swings every day. Work for 30 seconds, rest for 45 seconds, work again for 30 seconds. Do this five times, increasing it to seven times by week four. Also follow the same routine for the single-handed swing.

The golf bag lift should be carried out three times a week. Halve your time from the pre-training and do that time in three repetitions so if your time was 20 you now want to do 3 × 10 lifts. Take a minute rest in between lifts. Gradually increase the number of repetitions to five by the end of four weeks.

In addition to the above the following exercises for suppleness should be carried out every day.

(a) Neck rolling in both directions, then touch each shoulder alternately with the chin, and finally touch chest with chin.

(b) Arm circling: keep arms straight and rotate each in turn.

(c) Bend the trunk sideways as far as possible. Alternate the side it bends towards.

(d) Leg stretches: keep legs wide apart and straight. With palms of hands slide down the outside of one leg as far as possible and then down the other.

(e) Sit on floor with legs apart and straight. With arms folded try to touch floor with elbows.

(f) To develop the hamstring stand upright with your legs straight and feet crossed. Push down with your hands to touch your feet. Keep swapping feet over.

(g) Leg stretching to develop the calf. Place legs apart with one foot well in front of the other. Put your weight on the front leg and with your heels on the floor pull the calf of the rear leg. Alternate with right and left leg in forward position.

(h) Skip jumps on the spot.

(i) Spot running.

With these exercises you will feel strain. But take your time; don't rush them. Only the last two need to be carried out with anything like pace.

You are probably thinking this sounds like an awful lot of hard work just to play golf. But don't worry, it always looks worse written down on paper than it actually is.

After carrying out that programme for a month you will notice a marked improvement in your performance. Go through your pre-fitness test again and compare your new figures with your old ones four weeks ago. You'll be surprised, and, furthermore, will appreciate what the exercise programme has done for you.

You must set yourself goals when carrying out training and if you keep a record of how you are doing then you can see the benefits from your efforts and hard work.

Now that you have got through the first four weeks I'm sure you are beginning to enjoy it and are wanting to extend your programme.

You should now aim to increase your targets. Look at your progression in the first four weeks and realistically draw up a further programme of planned expansion and increase. Don't get too optimistic though.

With your running schedule, rather than increase your distances, time yourself over a set run and then try and do a greater distance in the same time and gradually push this distance up. Let's say you can cover 4 miles (6km) in 25 minutes, try and increase it to 5 miles (8km) in 25 minutes. And so on. To·make the fast running programme tougher, apart from increasing the distances between the markers, you could put them on a slight hill.

The body exercises (sit-ups etc) can be made harder purely by increasing the number of repetitions.

You can include some of your own exercises if you wish. But remember to make sure they are all related to golf. And finally, remember that golf is fun. Your fitness training should also be fun. But it will hurt at times. There again, so does golf!

FIFTEEN

GOLFING INJURIES

Fortunately golfers don't come up against the sort of injuries tennis players, footballers, squash players, etc encounter. In fact, there are very few injuries that golfers sustain. Of course, it is possible to break a leg playing golf, but if you insist on doing something stupid like climbing a tree to recover a ball then what can you expect? most injuries sustained on a golf course are through negligence rather than the strain of the sport.

In the long term, people who play golf regularly can expect some form of wear and tear on their body and joints because of excessive swinging. The back is the biggest source of attack after years of golf, as well as the knees and elbow joints. But don't read into it that you will become crippled as a result of playing golf ... you won't.

Talking of backs. You must remember you do a lot of bending in a game of golf. You bend at least 36 times, probably more, so you must be careful and ensure you bend properly.

Probably the biggest cause for concern on the golf course is people being injured by flying golf balls, as happened in the 1989 British Open at Troon. The cry of *Fore*! must always be made if your ball appears to be heading for another player or bystander. *Fore*! probably came to be a golfing exclamation from the military command of 'Beware Before!', which was mentioned by Scottish reformer John Knox in the 16th century as a command to troops to fall to the ground so that gunfire would pass over them. It is amazing how people instinctively duck or protect themselves upon this cry, and thus reduce the risk of injury. Injuries are often caused by players being impatient with parties in front of them, and playing their shot too soon. Make sure player(s) in front of you are well out of range before you play your next shot.

Most golfers take practice swings either on the fairway or on the side of the tee. Make sure there is nobody within range of your club.

SIXTEEN

PROFESSIONAL STYLE

Having taken you through all aspects of this great game, it is worth looking at some of the world's outstanding players to see how they play the game.

We emphasized at the very beginning how important it is to work to a 'blue-print'. All professional golfers adhere to that blue-print, but many have their own characteristics which make them distinguishable, and that helps to make golf a great game to watch.

Paul Azinger

Paul Azinger's strong left-hand grip and upright swing is a perfect example of how individual styles can be successful. Azinger has been one of the 'finds' on the US tour in the last three years and owes a great deal of his success to his putting technique.

Severiano Ballesteros

Spain's leading golfer, Sevvy has been one of the world's top golfers throughout the eighties and has won Majors in both Britain and America. An interesting style point is the early cocking of his wrists, but at the same time he has a magnificent pivot. We have seen many times that he is the master of all shots and can even play them from car parks!

Mark Calcavecchia

Mark Calcavecchia can be described as America's version of 'The Great White Shark' – Greg Norman. He attacks everything, as British fans saw when he won the Open in 1989. Calcavecchia is just one of many golfers who highlight how athletic the game of golf has become in recent years.

Ben Crenshaw

The modern day professional plays the game under great pressure. Ben Crenshaw is a player who has maintained the sportsmanlike image of golf despite playing under those conditions. Very popular with the British fans, he has a full swing, but the hallmark of his game has been his consistent putting.

Laura Davies

Britain's Laura Davies has established herself as one of the great women golfers and proved that she can take on and beat the Americans in their own back yard. She is capable of winning on any golf course

Bernhard Langer is the first truly great West German golfer.

anywhere in the world. She has tremendous power and can hit the golf ball a long way.

Nick Faldo

Britain's Nick Faldo underwent a major 're-designing' of his swing a couple of years ago and it paid immediate dividends in the shape of the British Open and US Masters titles. If you examine his swing closely you will see how parallel to the ball-to-target line he keeps the club at the top of the back swing.

Mark James

Mark James' attitude is one of complete professionalism. He fears nobody and that was shown in 1989 by his many successes. He has a very individual style but it is consistent, and that has maintained his winning ways.

Tom Kite

In recent years Tom Kite has probably been the most consistent money winner on the US tour without winning the Major titles. He is third on the all-time money list behind Tom Watson and Jack Nicklaus, which highlights his level of consistency. A steady golfer, he doesn't attract the media attention like some of his counterparts but just gets on with the job. ·

Bernhard Langer

Bernhard Langer is an example of what dedication and mental and physical effort can achieve. He has overcome major problems in the last couple of years to re-confirm his standing as one of Europe's top golfers. On his day there is no finer medium-iron golfer in the world. Like Nick Faldo, Langer's resurgence is an example of 'back to basics'.

Sandy Lyle

Tremendously talented, Sandy Lyle is truly an international golfer and has won tournaments on all continents. When required he can hit the golf ball further than any of his rivals.

Jack Nicklaus

Jack Nicklaus is probably the most complete golfer ever seen. Nobody has come close to challenging his superiority and his total of 18 professional Majors is likely to remain unbeaten for a long time. Strength of character and dedication are two of Jack's biggest assets. When he first appeared on the scene nearly 30 years ago he was an exceptionally long hitter and he showed the benefits of hitting the ball a long way. Today it is just expected that the professional golfer should hit the ball those distances.

Greg Norman

Australian Greg Norman is a fine example of a golfer with determination. He is a great competitor and has tremendous power. He is one of the bravest shot-makers around and has a complete all-round game, but sadly he has not won as many titles as he has threatened to do in recent years. Like many players before him, he learned his 'trade' on the European tour before being lost to the US tour.

Jose-Maria Olazabal

Olazabal is a fine example of the younger breed of modern-day professional golfer. He is a magnificent competitor and has a superb short game. Like most other professionals he is an excellent shot-maker which is crucial in the world of professional golf these days.

A straight left arm as demonstrated by Chip Beck
during the epic 1989 Ryder Cup at the Belfry.

A 'hand and arm' pitch from hard ground by Ian
Woosnam during the Volvo P.G.A. at Wentworth, 1989.

Payne Stewart

One of the biggest attributes of Payne Stewart is his ability to raise his game on the big occasions as shown in 1989 when he won the US PGA championship, his first Major, after a few near misses. Stewart realizes the entertainment value of golf (you only have to look at the way he dresses!) and takes full advantage.

Ronan Rafferty

Irishman Rafferty is a fine example of a golfer who has benefited from practice and dedication. He has always had a sound game but he realized that to do well on the European tour he needed to practice regularly. It is now paying dividends as he has become a fine international player with real commitment.

Curtis Strange

The most outstanding American golfer to emerge in recent years, he owes a great deal of his success to a change in attitude. But Curtis Strange is, and always has been, a very fine golfer and is the perfect example of how one should employ a good full shoulder turn on the backswing.

Tom Watson

A fine aggressive striker of the golf ball, Tom Watson is loved and admired by the British public and in 1989 was in contention for the British Open title. Even at this fairly late stage of his career Tom Watson is still seeking advice from coaches in an effort to improve his game. For the man who has won more money from the sport than any other, there has got to be something to be learnt from that ...

Ian Woosnam

For a small man Ian Woosnam generates tremendous power. The secret of his success is the ease with which he generates that power. He will go on winning for many years. Stand next to Woosnam when he is driving; it is an awesome experience.

TWO · NEWCOMERS
TO · LOOK · OUT · FOR

Russell Claydon

Russell made the transition from the amateur game to the professional ranks in 1989 and immediately showed his great talent. He is another example of how an individual style can be successful. He also has great strength.

Vijay Singh

The first Fijian golfer to make an impact, he won his first European tour event in 1989. Very tall, he naturally has an upright swing. But his biggest attribute is his ability to work hard at his game. Such devotion will reap further rewards in the future.

All the above golfers are great shot-makers, as indeed all professional golfers are these days. But they have only gained that ability by sheer dedication and hard work. Nothing comes easy in this life. And playing winning golf is certainly something that must be worked hard at if success is to be attained.

TESTING TIME

A series of question, and answers, to see how much you have learned on the foregoing pages.

1. Which fingers of your left hand should apply pressure to the club handle when adopting your normal hold:
   (a) All five fingers
   (b) Your last three fingers
   (c) Your thumb, forefinger and little finger

2. ... And which fingers of the right hand should apply pressure?
   (a) Your thumb and forefinger
   (b) All five fingers
   (c) Your second and third fingers

3. In the hold, where should the 'Vs' formed by your two hands both be pointing?
   (a) To a point midway between your face and right shoulder
   (b) Towards your right shoulder
   (c) Towards your face

4. When playing a wooden club should the ball be in line with:
   (a) Your left toe
   (b) Left heel
   (c) Right heel

5. When adopting a normal square stance are:
   (a) Your heels parallel to the ball-to-target line
   (b) Your toes parallel to the ball-to-target line

6. To allow a good pivot when playing a wooden club is it advisable to:
   (a) adopt a slightly square stance
   (b) adopt a slightly closed stance
   (c) adopt an open stance

7. What causes the takeaway?
   (a) The arms and elbows moving backwards
   (b) The right shoulder and hip moving backwards slightly
   (c) The knees bending to the right

8. At the top of the backswing where should your right elbow be pointing?
   (a) At the ground just behind your right heel
   (b) At the target
   (c) AT your right knee

9. ... and at the top of the backswing, where should the shaft of the club be pointing?
   (a) At the ball
   (b) Parallel to the ball-to-target line
   (c) To the right of the target

10. On the downswing, which part of your body comes through first?
    (a) Hands
    (b) Legs
    (c) Hips

11. Which of the following is the most important part of the downswing?
- **(a)** Maintaining a steady head and spinal angle
- **(b)** Keeping a good straight left arm
- **(c)** Transferring your weight from one leg to the other properly

12. When using your driver how high should you tee your ball?
- **(a)** So that half the ball shows above the top of the club-head
- **(b)** So that at least half of the ball shows above the top of the club-head
- **(c)** So that slightly less than half of the ball is showing above the club-head

13. How would you describe a 6-iron?
- **(a)** Long iron
- **(b)** Medium iron
- **(c)** Short iron

14. Why is it necessary to open your stance slightly when playing short irons?
- **(a)** Because the swing is short and less body movement is required
- **(b)** To compensate for a tendency to slice short iron shots
- **(c)** To allow for the extra loft on the club

15. Which of the following are possible causes of a slice?
- **(a)** club-face open at address
- **(b)** one or both hands too far to the right on the handle
- **(c)** Ball positioned too far back at address
- **(d)** Club face rolled open at the start of the backswing
- **(e)** Club taken away on the outside, creating an out-to-in swing path

16. ... and which of the following are possible causes of the hook?

- **(a)** Club-face closed at address
- **(b)** Ball positioned too far back at address
- **(c)** Hands too far forward at address
- **(d)** Club pointing to the right of the target at the top of the backswing
- **(e)** Right elbow and upper arm held too close to body in the back and downswing

17. Which of the following is a possible cause of topping?
- **(a)** Ball too far forward at address
- **(b)** Ball too close to your feet
- **(c)** Bodyweight not shifting to left leg on the backswing

18. When playing an uphill lie should you:
- **(a)** take a more lofted club than the shot would normal require
- **(b)** take a less lofted club
- **(c)** take the same club as you would if playing the shot off level ground

19. When playing a downhill lie there is a tendency to create an out-to-in swing path. Should you therefore:
- **(a)** Aim slightly to the left of the target
- **(b)** Close your stance
- **(c)** Aim slightly to the right of the target

20. When playing out of long uncut grass should you:
- **(a)** Take a wooden club
- **(b)** Take a long iron
- **(c)** Take a short iron

21. When playing a ball 'sitting up' in light rough what is the most important thing to do?
- **(a)** Adopt a steep angle of attack on the ball
- **(b)** Shorten the hold on the handle
- **(c)** Open your stance

GOLF

22. Where should you position the ball at address when playing a pitch shot?
    (a) At a point mid-way between your two feet
    (b) slightly right of centre
    (c) slightly left of centre

23. When chipping you should attempt to take the loft off the club. How is this achieved?
    (a) By holding your hands slightly forward at address
    (b) By holding the club further down the handle
    (c) By moving the ball further back in the address position

24. Where should you fix your eyes when playing a bunker shot?
    (a) On the top of the ball

    (b) at a point about 2 in (5 cm) behind the ball
    (c) at a point about 2 in (5 cm) in front of the ball

25. When playing a ball plugged in a bunker should you:
    (a) Adopt an open stance with open club-face
    (b) Adopt a closed stance with open club-face
    (c) Adopt a square stance with closed club-face

26. To encourage a top-spin strike of the ball when putting, where should the ball be positioned in relation to your feet?
    (a) Opposite your left foot
    (b) Opposite your right foot
    (c) Between your two feet

ANSWERS

1. (b) The last three fingers
2. (c) Your second and third fingers
3. (a) To a point mid-way between your face and right shoulder
4. (b) Your left heel
5. (a) Your heels parallel to the ball-to-target line
6. (b) adopt a slightly closed stance
7. (b) The right shoulder and hip moving backwards slightly
8. (a) At the ground just behind your right heel
9. (b) Parallel to the ball-to-target line
10. (c) Hips
11. All three are important but (a) maintaining the head and spinal angle is probably the most important
12. (b) So that at least half of the ball shows above the top of the club-head
13. (b) Medium iron
14. (a) Because the swing is short and less body movement is required
15. **(a)** club-face open at address, **(d)** Club face rolled open at the

start of the backwsing, and **(e)** Club taken away on the outside creating an out-to-in swing path, are all possible causes of the slice.

16. All five are possible causes of the hook
17. (a) Ball too far forward at address
18. (b) take a less lofted club
19. (a) Aim slightly to the left of target
20. (c) Take a short iron. You need to use a club with a heavy head and also with sufficient loft to get the ball out. Don't be afraid to use your sand wedge in such situations
21. (b) Shorten the hold on the handle
22. (c) slightly left of centre
23. (a) By holding your hands slightly forward at address
24. (b) at a point about 2 in (5 cm) behind the ball
25. (c) Adopt a square stance and closed club-face
26. (a) Opposite your left foot

GLOSSARY

Ace: A hole in one.
Address: The position assumed when a player is about to make a stroke.
Air shot: A stroke failing to make contact with the ball.
Albatross: A score of three under par on one hole.
American tournament: A competition in which every golfer plays everyone else.
Apron: Close-cut grass on the fairway bordering the green.
Arc: The path of the clubhead through the air during the swing.
As it lies: A ball must be played from where it comes to rest, unless the rules allow it to be moved.
Away: The ball furthest from the hole, which is played first.
Back marker: The player with the lowest handicap in a match or competition.
Backspin: reverse spin which makes the ball fly high and stop quickly.
Bisque: A handicap stroke which can be used any time in a match.
Block: The lack of hip movement which prevents the clubface from striking the ball correctly, resulting in a push or slice.
Borrow: The path of a putt aimed to one side to compensate for the slope of the green.
Break: The sideways movement of a ball when putted across a slope.
Carry: The distance a ball travels through the air.
Casual water: Temporary extra, unplanned water on the course.
Chip: A low shot to the green which rolls for most of its journey.
Choke down: taking a lower grip or the club than normal.
Closed face: When the clubface points left of the target.
Closed stance: When a player's feet are directed right of the target.
Clubhead: The part of the club which strikes the ball.

Cocking the wrists: The bend of the wrists during the backswing.
Cup: Another word for the hole.
Cut: Hitting a ball with sidespin.
Dog leg: A hole with a sharp bend between tee and green.
Dormy: A player is dormy in matchplay when he is as many holes up as there are left to be played. He cannot be beaten unless the match goer to extra holes.
Double bogey: Two over par for a hole.
Double eagle: American term for Albatross.
Draw: A slightly hooked shot.
Drop: If his ball goes out of bounds, is lost or unplayable, the player drops a ball back into play.
Face: The part of the clubhead which strikes the ball.
Fade: A shot struck to drift sideways towards the target, avoiding a hazard.
Flat swing: A swing in which the club is carried on a low plane around the body.
Flight: The path of the ball through the air.
Follow through: The swing arc after striking the ball.
Fore!: Traditional warning shouted when the ball is flying towards another person.
Free drop: A drop without penalty, such as away from casual water or ground under repair.
Frost holes: Temporary greens used to avoid damage to normal greens during icy weather.
Grip: The club shaft cover. The hold of the hands on the club.
Grain: Blades of grass lying horizontally rather than standing up.
Gross: A player's score before his handicap is deducted.
Head up: Lifting the head top quickly during or after the strike.
Hole: The target on each green. Always four and a quarter inches in diameter, and four inches deep.

Honour: The right to play first from the tee.

Hood: Reducing the loft of the club by placing the hands ahead of the clubface.

Hook: A (mis)shot of which the flight bends right to left.

Interlocking grip: A grip in which the forefinger and little fingers are wrapped around each other to bind the hands together.

Lag: A cautious putt hit with the objective of getting near, rather than in, the hole.

Let through: Waving through the following game because of slower play or lost ball.

Lie: The position in which the ball comes to rest. The angle between the shaft and the bottom of the club.

Loft: The angle of slope on the clubface, which determines the height and distance the hit ball with travel.

Long game: Play with the woods and long irons.

Lost ball: A wayward ball unlocated after five minutes' search, or less if the player declares it lost.

Nap: The growth, direction, and general condition of the green.

Net score: A score after a player's handicap has been deducted.

Open: Competitions which anyone can enter, although there are usually some restrictions.

Open face: When the clubface is directed right of the target.

Open stance: The address when the feet point left of the target.

Par: The number of strokes a good player should take on a hole. Two shots are allowed for the green. Par threes are holes of up to 250 yards. Par fours are up to 475 yards, and the remainder are par fives.

Pin high: A ball which stops level with the flagstick.

Plane: The angle of the swing.

Plugged lie: A ball buried into the ground.

Pot bunker: A small bunker, usually round and deep.

Pro-am: A competition played by amateurs and professionals.

Pull: A straight shot left of the target.

Push: A straight shot right of the target.

Practice swing: This is allowed anywhere, provided there is no intention or likelihood of hitting the ball.

Quitting: Not following through a planned stroke.

Release: Free movement of the hands and arms at impact.

Reverse overlap grip: A putting grip in which the index finger of the top hand is placed over the fingers of the bottom hand.

Rub of the green: Accidental deflections of the ball.

Run: The distance the ball travels after it hits the ground.

Scratch: A no-handicap player.

Slice: A (mis)shot of which the flight curves from left to right.

Snap hook: A hook which bends very quickly.

Sole: The underside of the clubhead.

Square stance: placing the feet parallel with the target line.

Stance: The placing of the feet before a shot.

Sweet spot: The strongest part of the clubface, which will strike the ball furthest.

Take away: The beginning of the backswing.

Tee: The place from which the ball is driven at the start of each hole.

Texas wedge: A shot played with a putter from a position short of the green.

Thinning: Striking the ball with the bottom of the club.

Toe: The tip of the clubhead, furthest from the shaft.

Topping: Striking the top of the ball.

Topspin: Spin caused by striking the top of the ball.

Wedge: A pitching club with a low leading edge, producing exaggerated loft.

Wrist cocking: The natural breaking movement of the wrists during the backswing.

Wry-necked: description of putter with a pronounced curve in the neck.

INDEX

Page references in **bold** refer to photographs.

Also available in the Ward Lock
Ahead of the Game series:

TENNIS by L.T.A. Coach Anne Pankhurst 07063 6870 3

SQUASH by England international and S.R.A. Coach David Pearson 07063 6885 1

SOCCER by F.A. Coach Mike McGlynn 07063 6886 X